Oxtail Soup

Oxtail
Soup

for the Island Soul

Peter S. Adler

Ox Bow Press
Woodbridge, Connecticut

P.O. Box 4045
Woodbridge, CT 06525
203 387-5900; fax 203 387-0035
oxbow@gte.net

Composition: Windfall Software, using ZzTeX
Cover Art: Steve Underwood

Most of the stories contained in this book were published in their original form in *ISLANDS*, dated as follows: "The Back of Beyond," Sept./Oct. 1999; "The Neighbors Drop In," July/Aug. 1999; "Garden Fever," May/June 1999; "Shark Watch," Mar./Apr. 1999; "Sushi Man," Jan./Feb. 1999; "Tsunami Warnings," Nov./Dec. 1998; "Swinging in the Rain," Sept./Oct. 1998; "Swamp Creatures," July/Aug. 1998; "Frozen Fire," May/June 1998; "A Sense of Belonging," Mar./Apr. 1998; "Heart of Fire," Jan./Feb. 1998; "Heartbeats," Nov./Dec. 1997; "Breakfast in Paradise," Sept./Oct. 1997; "Flashing Paddles," July/Aug. 1997; "Harbor Moves," May/June 1997; "Ruff Water," Mar./Apr. 1997; "Into the Clouds: The Secret Side of Maui," Jan./Feb. 1997; "Hot Times," Nov./Dec. 1996; "Dawn Patrol," Sept./Oct. 1996; "Fish Central," July/Aug. 1996; "Traveler & Collector," May/June 1996; "Small Perfections," Mar./Apr. 1996; "Feed Willy," Jan./Feb. 1996. An early version of "Pig Wars" appeared in *Negotiation Journal*, July 1995.

Library of Congress Cataloging-in-Publication Data

Adler, Peter S., 1944–
    Oxtail soup for the island soul / Peter S. Adler.
        p.   cm.
    ISBN 1-8811987-20-5 (pbk. : alk. paper)
    1. Hawaii—Social life and customs.   1. Title.
DU624.5 A35 2001
996.9'042—dc21   2001021387

It is not necessary for a writer to be crazy, but it is useful.

—Anonymous

Contents

Preliminaries

I have a confession to make. For nearly three decades I have gone to elaborate, sometimes excessively cunning lengths to avoid that oppressive assemblage of household chores that every red-blooded twentieth-century family man is expected to do on Saturdays and Sundays. Instead of lawn mowing, sidewalk sweeping, car fixing, tree pruning, and gutter cleaning, I have ingeniously dissipated my weekends exploring life's off-the-beaten-path places in search of stories that illuminate the heart and soul of the place I live.

My cover for this has been that of a "writer," something I do for love and, by a strange twist of fate, occasionally get paid for. That was precisely my circumstance from early 1996 to late 1999 when I did a stint as a contributing editor to *ISLANDS* Magazine. For each issue, I produced a little column called "Postcard from Hawai'i." My mission, as handed to me by Editor Joan Tapper at the onset, was simple: check out the truth of the place I have the good fortune to call home, verify that real "aloha" still exists in the land of aloha, and then report the details back to those hundreds of thousands of Hawai'i-o-philes who, through no fault of their own, must spend the bulk of their days elsewhere.

A pleasurable enough process and a marvelous task if ever there was one. Joan called, I answered, we talked, we dick-ered a bit over financial and artistic matters, and then for several years I got to sleuth around the Islands poking my nose into the affairs of others and generally meddling in things that interested me. Most were matters I thought would interest oth-ers. As happened when I wrote *Beyond Paradise* in the early 1990s, my scrivener missions were filled with interesting peo-ple, odd encounters, and, on several occasions, the discovery of some especially bizarre things going on around me.

On the Big Island, for example, I spent several days with my old friends Russell and Anne Kokubun experiencing firsthand a condition that I can only call "Boar-a-phoria" and in a place that will, for me, forevermore be thought of as the real Hog Heaven. Wandering around on Lāna'i looking for a certain nature preserve, I found a different kind of Nirvana: the happy hunting ground of World War II Jeeps. A mile from my house on O'ahu I discovered three little patches of forest and garden that seemed to encapsulate so much of what is precisely right about Hawai'i. On Maui, I stumbled around in a mountain bog with a Snail Man. And on Kaua'i, I looked deeply into the eyes of a monster and found we were related.

All of this provided adventure, challenge, and stimulation. Captains James T. Kirk and Jean-Luc Picard of "Star Trek" fame never had it so easy. Wandering around the nooks, crannies, and odd corners of the 50th State has been, and continues to be, a most joyful task. More important, I have learned that all my elaborate and complex scheming and strategizing were completely unnecessary. You don't have to sneak up on the real Hawai'i because it exists in everyday things. It grounds and surrounds you from the moment you wake up until that very specific nanosecond when the stars blink off, your eyelids close, and sleep envelopes you.

Moving around the Islands also reaffirmed much of what I knew beforehand, that life in Hawai'i is composed of many small everyday dramas and that like anyplace else, it is a mix of the good and the bad. I met Hawaiian men and women, some of whom prefer to be called by the older term *"kanaka maoli,"* a term I have tried to honor, and many of whom are bemoaning the loss of their ancient culture even as their children actually recover it. I talked with hard-working immigrants from Vietnam and Cambodia who put a hundred hours a week into their storefront businesses so that they can send their sons and daughters to college. I found fourth- and fifth-generation local families celebrating their private histories, and former Peace Corps volunteers in Malaysia and India who have settled here and are making new histories that will be remembered five generations from now.

My investigations sometimes touched sensitive nerves. While the rest of the United States enjoyed a period of expansive growth during the 1990s, Hawai'i's economy was in recession. First, the Gulf War deflated Hawai'i's tourism sector. Then our struggling sugar and pineapple industries folded their tents. Finally, Japanese investment slowed to a trickle. Lacking opportunities in the Islands, many young people left for New York, Seattle, and Los Angeles.

All of this created a dark undercurrent of worry that came out after the initial pleasantries wore off when I spoke with people. The woman who runs the little boutique in Mānoa Valley thought she might have to close her clothing store. Two of the places mentioned in the pages that follow, Fresh Market and Columbia Inn, actually did close. The guy working the lunch counter in the bowling alley near Kamehameha Shopping Center fretted about break-ins and property thefts. Even the governor was grumpy when I met with him in his chambers at the State Capitol. "It's all changing . . . " he said, letting his words drift off.

Other contradictions came to the fore. Though Hawai'i's public, private, and civic leaders rarely speak about it openly, our smiling and friendly ways are sometimes deceptive. Not unlike other places, local politics and local business braid together and when things get tough, they turn into brass knuckled back-room affairs. Here, however, it seems unexpected. One observer said that Hawai'i combines the worst political traits of Louisiana and Japan. Regardless, wherever I went and whoever I talked to, Hawai'i's changing demographics, sagging productive power, and fierce politics were much on people's mind. At least at first . . . .

Very quickly, no matter how grim things seemed to be on the front page of the paper, the other Hawai'i—the REAL Hawai'i—would come back in focus. As it always does—and as it always will. But the reminders were always interesting. In one instance it was a junior park ranger in Hawai'i Volcanoes National Park who thrilled me with her elation at being near the raw, fiery energy that courses through our subterranean geological arteries. In another, it was a shark researcher from the University of Hawai'i who spends most of his time on a boat following turquoise ocean currents that shimmer and sparkle as they pour swell after swell on our shores. And on a different day, it was Nainoa Thompson, chief navigator of the deep-water, open-ocean sailing canoe *Hōkūle'a,* who talked to me about the revitalization of local culture through sea journeys to Easter Island, New Zealand, and the Marquesas, voyages that haven't been done for 1,500 years.

So it comes down to this. Life in the Islands isn't perfect, but on any given day you can bank on the fact that it's better than in most other places. Our green rain forests will be resonating with primeval heat and humidity. The air will be redolent with the smell of ginger, *pakalana,* and frangipani.

It is axiomatic that you will find the ocean and the mountains accessible when you need to refresh yourself or follow some special trail of discovery that connects your inner and outer geographies. At the beginning of each day you will see people of Eastern, Western, and Oceanic ancestries swirling together and creating their own cultural alchemy beneath a sky that is rife with the possibility of rainbows. And at the end of the day, you will remember the little domesticities that make life on an island in the Hawaiian archipelago so different and distinct. This book celebrates what makes us so different from the rest of the world.

In Polynesia, as in the traditional cultures of Asia and Europe where my people come from, courtesy and protocol are everything. First on the list of people to be acknowledged are those who inhabit the stories that follow and who allowed me into their lives—a rare and honored privilege. In no particular order, the list includes, among many others, Sam Ahai, Ryoko Ishii, Dave Lyman, Alan Thoma, Alan Sandrey, Don and Anna Womack, Bailey Kuewa, the Watanabe clan (Tetsui, Alice, KC, Gail, Keri, Bryce, Reid, Brent, Julie, Ian, Erin, Roger, Carol, Alyssa, Jessica, Tom, Kathy, Sarah, Laura, and Grandma Ruth), Bob Hobdy, Mike Severns, Jerry Crowe, Kim Holland, Russ and Anne Kokubun, Don Leong, Claire Matsumoto, Joyce Matsumoto (no relation to Claire), Yves Garnier and the cooks and servers at La Mer, Neal Milner, Kem and Junko Lowry, Masa Nakayama, Sam and Mary Cooke (and their now departed 1990 Jaguar), Tom and Wilma Ogimi, John Barkai, Linda Martel, Tink Ashford, Frank Damon, Keith Hunter, Dan Walker, Chip McCreery, Kenny and Chizuko Endo, Alenka Remec, Brian Valley, Hiʻilei Silva, Ellen Carson, Brad and Sachi Coates, Gaylord and Carol Wilcox, Kent Davis, Elizabeth Kent, and Kent Preiss-Davis (these last three being all in the same family), Coach Harry, Hiroko, Cow Man, Pig Man, and Laundromat Larry.

Most especially, I want to thank those who tolerated, inspired, motivated, and helped with the task. Joan Tapper, editor of *ISLANDS* and several other lovely international magazines, gave me the original opportunity and incentive to write these pieces and permission to bring them together as a book. Lucille Stein, the plucky and ever-energetic publisher of Ox Bow Press, pushed me to finish the project. Sam Gon, a biologist and native speaker of the Hawaiian language at The Nature Conservancy, and Lani Maʻa Lapilio, director of the Hawaii Judicial History Center, read and critiqued the draft for Hawaiian content and spelling. Eileen D'Araujo corrected mistakes and found dozens of ways to improve the manuscript. Bryce Watanabe, my nephew, conceptualized the artwork. Corey, Dana, and Kelly Adler, my daughters who are dearer to me than life and who populate some of the stories that follow, supported the effort with unconditional understanding and love. Most of all, I thank my bride of 30+ years, Carolyn Watanabe, who saw right through all of my chore-skipping behavior as if I was the invisible man and told me to "go for it" anyway.

A Broth of Islands

D r. Robert Putnam, a distinguished professor of international affairs at Harvard University, has an interesting theory. In a broad-ranging inquiry into the decline of civic engagement and social capital in America, he has found that although more people than ever are going bowling, organized bowling has declined significantly. He thinks that individualized activities like this are a symptom of the deteriorating fabric of community. Americans, he argues in a book of the same title, are "bowling alone."

Insightful as his observation may be, Putnam has obviously never visited the Kamehameha Bowling Alley in Honolulu. If he had, his theory might have taken a different trajectory. He would inevitably have seen that social bowling springs eternal in the local soul. Nestled into the Kalihi neighborhood in Honolulu's urban core, Kamehameha Bowl, known more colloquially as "Kam Bowl," has more than twenty lanes that clatter, smack, and thunk with the sound of flying pins and gutter balls morning, noon, and night. Most of the bowlers who come to Kam Bowl are regulars and they have been enjoyably hurling balls in clubs and leagues for years.

Bowling, however, is slightly incidental to our mission. As it happens, the coffee shop inside the Kamehameha Bowling Alley is famous for its oxtail soup, and Louie Chang and I have come here with the sole goal of having some. Oxtail soup is special stuff. Other hole-in-the-wall eateries serve it, but Kam Bowl's is widely regarded as the best. If you don't believe me, do your own survey. Ask Honolulu people where they go for this little gem and you will inevitably hear about the College Walk Inn, Wisteria, and Liberty Grill. So too King's Cafe, Masa's, Columbia Inn, the Fremont Hotel in Las Vegas where a lot of local people go to gamble, and—one day a week and at lunch time only—the cafeteria in the Board of Water Supply Building kitty-corner from the State Capitol. Invariably, Kam Bowl's name rises to the top of the list.

It is also a cultural intertidal zone with a common bovine denominator. Each day a small herd of cows contributes its collective posterior anatomy to the cause. Each day, between 7 A.M. and 11 P.M., Kam Bowl's cooks stir a quarter ton of these tails into giant vats of broth. Each day a dozen waitresses shuttle back and forth from the kitchen to the dining area taking and bringing orders and chatting with customers. And each day nearly a thousand local residents, all differing by age, class, gender, ethnicity, and body morphology, troop into Kam Bowl to ooh and aah over this delectable stuff.

Louie, my navigator and chief adviser and counselor on this (and many other matters), is an esteemed colleague, a neighbor, and one of my closest friends. A quiet, soft-spoken, and exceedingly competent attorney, he takes serious interest in food and cookery. Moreover, he is extremely knowledgeable in these matters. Some of this is from careful research. He explores all manner of little hidey-hole restaurants around town, reads widely about the foods he gets interested in, and then tests them at home. Some of it, however, has to be from his Chinese heritage. I tend not to hold many stereotypes about people, but I own up to two: all Chinese are outstanding Ping-Pong players and they are all fixated on eating.

Under Lou's instructive and supervisory eye, this has led to some amazing culinary adventures. Over the last few years on work-related trips to America, we intentionally undertook a quest to find the world's best key lime pie. Excellent candidates have been discovered near Dupont Circle in D.C. and at a rib joint we stumbled onto by accident near Cape Canaveral where the astronauts hang out. In Baltimore, we intentionally hunted down and then relished the most succulent soft-shelled crabs on the planet. And in the dark, alien territory of Los Angeles, we traversed hostile freeways and dangerous neighborhoods to find titanic burritos that Lou had caught wind of from a friend of a friend.

Now, it is oxtail soup that tends to be humble, underrated, and not well appreciated by people with big-city taste buds. Most likely it is the idea of eating the stern end of an ox. What New Yorkers, Miamians, and Chicagoans don't know, of course, is that oxtail soup is a delicacy, a local comfort food that mixes subtle flavors, ancient memories, powerful condiments, and the traditions of immigrant plantation workers from China, Japan, Korea, and the Philippines. Oxtail soup is like Hawai'i itself, a steaming broth of tropical islands, of people who all originally came from some other place, of complex microclimates and subtle landscapes, of storied histories, of time-tested customs, and of peculiar dreams. All of this is stirred together in ways that attract the eye, please the palate, and soothe the soul.

Warnings are in order, of course. Anyone with low-calorie, dietary leanings will do well to avoid Kam Bowl. Yes, of course it is possible to order a side salad or fruit cup there, but no one does. Fundamentally, Kam Bowl is for meat-a-saurus kinds of people. Vegetarians and herbivores, those who philosophically refuse to eat creatures with faces, and those who are looking for vitamin supplements and grass juice energizers should just stay away. In fact, they should probably not even come to Hawai'i, which has the highest per capita consumption of canned Vienna sausages and Spam in the United States. In Hawai'i, people tend to enjoy the meat of many different animals. We use pork and chicken as a substitute for other ingredients, and we live by Redd Foxx's admonition that one day all the health nuts in the world are going to feel mighty stupid lying in the hospital dying of nothing.

As it turns out, however, oxtail soup is well regarded in many climes. The Vietnamese have a recipe that is built around noodles. Germans cook veal tails into a colloidal solution of onions, diced carrots, tomatoes, bay leaves, thyme, and celery and then add a large snort of Madeira. In the English version (which no one else in the world would touch), you peel and slice turnips and throw in some ground mace, flour, and mushroom ketchup. Then you augment the whole mess with copious amounts of ham and port wine. In Hawai'i, of course, oxtail soup has evolved from many different cultures. Not unlike the people who live here, it has mingled its way into something lighter and infinitely more graceful.

At the Kamehameha Bowling Alley, Lou and I settle onto two revolving stools at the end of the counter and look around. The coffee shop holds about fifty people. More people are waiting near the entrance for a table to clear. Next to us, a party of five very large men and women of mixed Asian, Polynesian, and European heritages are on their noon break. With the clack of pins in the background, they are talking and laughing and heartily spooning large amounts of soup into their mouth.

At the table next to them are three Japanese repairmen from an elevator company. All three are wearing dark green work shirts with white pocket protectors stuffed with pens, pencils, and little rulers and tools. They are working on their bowls of soup with the same quiet and concentrated intensity that I hope they use when they fix the elevator in my building. Meanwhile, a whiff of cigar smoke comes wafting in from the bowling alley. Kam Bowl may be the very last public place in the United States of America that allows smoking in general and cigars in particular. None of which is deterring the soup eaters.

Then there is the soup itself. The essence of oxtail cookery is disarmingly simple, but it must be done right. You trim the excess fat off the slices of tail, wash them, then drain the water. Once they are clean and all the scum has been removed, you cover them with boiling water. If you prefer, you can brown the tails in a saucepan first. If you are smart, you stop here, let the soup cool overnight, skim off any remaining fat, and reheat it the next morning. You add crushed ginger and garlic and maybe some mustard cabbage. Maybe some green onions, dried mushrooms, or pieces of squash. For flavor, you add dried tangerine peel, salt, pepper, Ajinomoto or star anise. Then you invite your friends and neighbors over (including Grandma Arizumi from across the street who used to run a restaurant in the neighborhood and who takes special pride in her own version). Then you eat.

At the counter, two gents sitting immediately to the left of Louie are stirring their soup and quietly debating the merits of their new cars, respectively a Honda and a Toyota. They have their aloha shirts tucked into their crisply pressed pants and look like downtown guys, most likely bankers or insurance agents, though they could be middle managers from the Department of Land and Natural Resources or the City and County's Motor Vehicle Bureau. Next to them, a stunning and elegantly dressed Asian woman is also at the counter engrossed in the half-empty soup bowl in front of her.

She has a mysterious oval face with full lips and high, arching eyebrows. She is wearing a white flowered dress and several gold necklaces and bracelets. Louie and I speculate.

I say she is half Chinese and half Korean. Louie says she's Filipina and, because he is chief counselor on most matters legal, epicurean, and artistic, I defer to him for the moment but continue pondering this important aesthetic question. A lot of eyes (male and female) are watching her, but she pays them no mind. She is focused exclusively on the piece of oxtail delicately poised on the spoon in front of her. She is holding this with her left hand. With her right hand, she is ever so carefully and with great dexterity picking out tasty morsels of meat with her chopsticks and popping them in her mouth.

The counter waitress sidles up and says: "What'll it be, boys?" Louie, a man of few words, points to the bowls in front of the downtown gents sitting next to us and smacks his lips. Then he gets up and takes a quick walk through the restaurant, leaving me to my own fate.

While he is gone, I return to the business of ethnographic research on the sartorially splendid oval-faced Filipina-Chinese-Korean (or whatever) woman dressed in white. Ever so discreetly I watch her adroitly handle the spoon, the chopsticks, the rice, and her soup. During a brief pause, she looks up at me. (Or is it past me?) I smile, but she ignores me. I smile harder, but she turns back to the bowl in front of her, fiercely, happily, and full of obvious soup-lust.

A few minutes later, Lou walks back with his intelligence report: all but seven people in the restaurant are having oxtail soup. Of those who aren't, several are eating cheeseburgers, one is having chicken curry, and the rest have ordered the sliced beef tongue plate, which is served with rice, gravy, shiitake mushrooms, and bamboo shoots. Beef tongue plate is a Friday special. Pigs feet soup is the Monday and Thursday special. No one is eating salad.

Our waitress comes back moments later with steaming bowls of soup, a small round condiment dish of shredded ginger, a side bowl of rice, chopsticks, and flat-bottomed Oriental spoons. We mix a little chili pepper water and Kikkoman soy sauce into the ginger, drop some rice in the soup, and dig in. Kam Bowl's coffee shop makes oxtail soup in industrial quantities, but it is amazingly light and supple in its flavors.

So, idle conversation and sideways observations cease and we eat. Then we eat some more. And after a while, I'm thinking to myself: given enough pots of the right size and girth, given enough oxtails and rice, and given enough clean water to boil, we could feed all of Latin America on this stuff. In fact, if we fed a few bowls of Hawaiian oxtail soup to the leaders of Russia, America, China, the Congo, Israel, and Iraq, we would quickly have world peace (or at least a sudden outbreak of common sense). At the very least, everyone's bowling scores would improve.

Slurping our broth and gnawing on tail bones, I think of the feeding of the everyday nourishment of bodies, minds, and souls. Soup of all kinds is a human essential. A thousand years ago in Europe, medieval remedy books extolled the virtues of chicken soup for its soothing and restorative powers. In India when I was in the Peace Corps and sick as a dog with a tropical fever, Mrs. Harnakar fed me chili pepper and it cleared the bugs out of me in a night. Life itself, we are told, emerged from a primordial soup of proteinlike molecules after our planet cooled. And in Hawai'i, oxtail soup is ultimately all about the real Hawai'i.

Beyond the lei-bedecked images of Waikīkī, beyond the long string of TV shows shot on location in the 50th State, beyond all of these ephemeral and ever glitzy images lies a place full of real people. If you want to participate in this, look around at Kam Bowl and then join in as bones are sucked and consommé is slurped amidst the steady clatter of people bowling together.

2

Into the Clouds

Maui. Island of enchantment. Before the dawn of human time, it was the home of a sun-snaring demigod. In ancient times, it was ruled by a succession of warrior chiefs. In the 1800s, missionaries, cattle ranchers, and sugar planters came and sculpted the valleys into farms and plantations. In the twentieth century, people from Asia, the Pacific, and America would come to Maui and leave their footprints indelibly etched on the island. Most recently, the island has witnessed an invasion of Kentucky Fried Chickens, Dollar Rent-A-Cars, Pizza Huts, and Starbucks.

If you happen to be on the island of Maui and you develop a craving for something more original, try looking toward the western part of the island and then up. On a reasonably clear day, you will instantly see them. Mountains, dark and green and foreboding. Mountains that are seldom visited and scarcely known. Mountains shrouded in mists and covered with a dense and bewildering wilderness. Mountains plucked from the imagination or from some deep memory of our species when all of us lived closer to the earth.

As you gaze up at them, think about this. The West Maui mountains, 5,778 feet at their highest point, are the remnant of a single ancient volcano that has weathered into an exceptionally complex montane geography. There are deep valleys and impenetrable gorges, prehistoric craters and wet marshes, knife-edged ridges, and rushing streams. Perfect growing temperatures and an annual rainfall of close to 400 inches have carpeted the mountain with a lush rain forest. Most days, mists hug the valley floors and clouds shroud the top.

Now do one more thing. Check out a good map and study some of the mountains' detailed features. What you will see is a diverse and mysterious assortment of land forms. There's Pu'u Kukui, West Maui's highest spot; Hana'ula, another peak located not far away at the 4,616-foot level; and various deep valleys that are home to the headwaters of half a dozen streams. There is Violet Lake, a marshy area not far from the center of the mountains, and 'Eke Crater, a near-perfect circle of rock located at the source of an ancient lava flow.

Ironically, it is not stone that dominates these little-known peaks and valleys but water. In geological terms, the West Maui mountains are a giant sponge. Absorbed in, sloshing around, and trapped under the mountains' volcanic features are millions upon millions of gallons of pure, fresh water. Some say it is the sweetest water in the world. Even those who would quibble about matters like this admit to its purity. Regardless, the combination of watershed and isolation have created a dense, green home for some of the rarest animals and plants in the Pacific.

Because of this, most of the mountains' upper reaches are a restricted conservation area. People are not generally allowed in and few would want to go there anyway if they knew how wet and inhospitable the mountains really are. Occasionally, ranchers who graze cattle at lower elevations will enter the rain forest to search for a lost cow. Intrepid pig hunters go up there. But for most folks, the West Maui mountains are a strange and impassable complex of crags, bogs, and jungle. There are exceptions, however.

Meet Bob Hobdy and Mike Severns.

Hobdy, a tall, big-boned, gray-bearded man with a wide smile and an affable manner, is one of the island's resident experts on the West Maui mountains. A naturalist by profession, he works for the Division of Forestry and Wildlife and has an encyclopedic knowledge of West Maui's flora and fauna. Having grown up on the nearby island of Lāna'i, he has also been wandering in and out of Hawai'i's wilderness areas since he was a small boy. Now, at age 53, Hobdy regularly outhikes and outclimbs people half his age.

Severns (who tells me that Hobdy is actually half billy goat) is six inches shorter, wiry, and bristling with energy. He is a world-acclaimed photographer, owner of a highly successful dive operation at nearby Kīhei, and a biologist with a particular fascination for mollusks. At age 46, Severns has swung down into West Maui's chasms from helicopters, poked into caves and lava tubes, discovered the bones of extinct birds (one of which is named after him), and mapped out the distribution, taxonomy, and morphology of several species of disappearing land snails.

Together, Hobdy and Severns share a deep passion for the mountains, an unwavering curiosity about Maui's animals and plants, and a fifteen-year history of rummaging through the drizzle-soaked backcountry trying to untangle the secrets of the cloud forest. Their quest has taken them to places most other people only know from tiny markings on topographic maps. And it has afforded me a unique opportunity to traipse along with them.

Early on a Saturday morning the three of us meet at a little general store at Mā'alaea Harbor, wolf down some hot dogs and Gatorade for breakfast, and then gather our boots and rain gear. Our plan is to take Mike's jeep and Bob's four-wheel-drive pickup, drive to McGregor Point on Maui's leeward side, unlock a fence, drive five miles straight up into the mountains, and then walk.

The potholed, boulder-strewn jeep road we are riding on follows the south rift of the original West Maui volcano. Bouncing around in the vehicles for an hour, we pass through progressively different vegetation zones. At sea level, where we start, we are in the rain shadow of the mountains. The land around us is a true desert, bone dry and covered with brown grasses. At this low elevation the mountains seem parched and angry with us for even contemplating an expedition to the higher reaches.

Then the desert merges into the low scrub typical of Hawai'i's dry lowland forest. Small *wiliwili* trees grow out of the sparse soils in the cracks of prehistoric lava flows. A short while later, we pass gnarled, windswept mesquite trees and then, above the open slope at 1,200 feet near some rock outcroppings, we encounter the first native forest plants.

We find *a'ali'i,* sacred to the ancient dancers of hula. There is the drooping, shiny-leaved *'ākia,* some species of which are poisonous, and *pūkiawe,* used in ancient fumigation rituals. We find dwarf *'ōhi'a lehua,* the beautiful red-blossomed tree associated with the volcano goddess, Pele, and then, as we gain elevation, the taller, denser *'ōhi'a* trees that characterize so many of Hawai'i's wet forests.

Lurching and jolting our way up the mountain, we pass long, rolling swales of green grass and, as we approach the rain forest, we startle a huge native owl out of his perch in a *koa* tree. Even as the owl flaps off in irritation, we suddenly find ourselves above the heat and in the spreading cool of the West Maui forest. The temperature is lower by ten degrees and the ground is damp. Large volcanic domes, jagged peaks, razorback ridges, and deep ravines surround us. Fog hangs in one of the valleys. Finally, where the road ends, we park our vehicles, lace up our boots, and with great anticipation start to walk.

Twenty paces up the skinny path that has been stamped out by wild pigs and semidomesticated visiting naturalists, Bob stops and immediately starts poking around in the underbrush. "Botanizing" is what forestry people call this. Poking around is what I call it. Mainly, it's identifying plants and examining the details of their location, range, health, and variation. Hobdy has a keen memory and a seemingly inexhaustible store of knowledge about the trees, shrubs, flowers, and fruits of the West Maui mountains. As we work our way up through the forest, he points out delicate native ferns, a rare terrestrial orchid called *Platanthera* (no more than a dozen of which are left), and various members of the sedge, primrose, and lobelia families, including a *Lobelia hypoleuca* with long, delicate, stunningly azure flowers. Bob knows them all. They are old friends, creatures he cares deeply about.

Severns is also no slouch when it comes to local plant lore, but his main interests lie in a genus of colorful endemic land snails called *Partulina,* small mollusks that have adapted to the unique rain forest conditions of each island. "I'm a snail man," he says with his thumb thumping his chest. "Him," he goes on with good-natured disdain as he crooks a finger at Hobdy, who is inspecting the underside of a large bush, "he's a plant guy." Severns is just as compulsive about snails as Hobdy is about plants and there is a steady good-natured banter that takes place between them as to whose area of interest is more important.

"Flora," says Hobdy, "is the basis of everything up here, including all those snails." Severns purses his lips and looks at Hobdy. "The problem with plants," he replies, "is they don't move. You got no behavior to watch." This kind of banter goes on for a quarter mile.

In fact, both of their interests converge fifty feet up the trail. Snail Man finds an old *'ōhi'a* tree and Plant Man, inspecting the underside of its leaves, locates a colony of *Partulina splendida*. Each little snail is dark brown with tan spiral bands. Mike, who comes up here every two or three months to map and photograph them, sometimes at night, has mounting evidence that most of these snails are variations of five basic species, some of whose shells spiral to the right, others to the left.

A mile up the trail, we start gaining more altitude. Every small ridge and valley in the West Maui mountains has its own regime of plants and animals. We work our way through thick tangles of brush along the side of a ravine, spot a crimson *'apapane,* a lovely red bird that is a member of the Hawaiian honeycreeper family, and then find ourselves in what naturalists call an "epiphytic" vegetation zone.

Epiphytes are plants that live on other plants. In the extreme wet areas that make up the heart of the cloud forest, lack of soil can be a limiting growth factor. Trees therefore become host habitats for dozens of species of vines, ferns, mushrooms, mosses, lichens, molds, and liverworts. Some of these plants are extraordinarily fragile and primitive. Bob points out a thin, filmy, epiphytic fern named *Vandenboschia davallioides* that is literally one cell thick. It is so highly adapted to moisture that it dies when there is too much sunshine. Even the insects that exist in this zone are dependent on specific plants for nourishment and camouflage and are incapable of living in other parts of the forest.

After several hours of clambering around on the ridges just below the summit of Hana'ula, we begin our descent. At an overlook in the very back of Ukumehame Valley, we look down several thousand feet from a high sheer spot and see two pairs of White-tailed Tropicbirds soaring on the currents. We discover tiny communities of mushrooms in the hollow parts of old logs, gardenias and greenswords, bright pink lobelias, several more native orchids, and—to Mike Severns' delight—more snails.

But the dark side is here also. All along the way we stop to pull out clumps of *Tibouchina,* an invasive plant species that was brought to the Hawaiian Islands from Brazil as an ornamental and that is now making its way into the heart of the West Maui mountains. A sprout here or there seems innocuous enough, but left to its own *Tibouchina* exudes a sticky sap that stains clothes black and can peel the skin off your hand. The danger is magnified by the fact that a single plant can give rise to a patch that is five acres wide and eight feet tall.

"Fifteen years from now," says Bob Hobdy with great sadness, "there is a very real likelihood that many of these magnificent native plants and animals that we are seeing will be gone." Without great vigilance, he explains, without more aggressive preservation and maintenance, invading species will overrun the valleys and ridges and eventually destroy the delicate balances that give such richness to the different vegetation zones of the West Maui mountains. Severns agrees. He worries that as key plants and trees are choked out, the isolated populations of land snails will inevitably disappear.

Conservation and education efforts are under way, however. The State of Hawai'i has designated four separate West Maui mountain tracts as "Natural Area Reserves," the goal of which is to preserve for perpetuity Hawai'i's most valuable pieces of forest. Private landowners are also involved. Large companies like Maui Land and Pineapple and AMFAC have forged partnerships with The Nature Conservancy and are carefully managing their lands to keep them pristine. Finally, there are Mike and Bob, who are describing and photographing what is up there for an educational book they are producing.

We squish our way through small bogs and muddy hollows, duck under fallen trees, stop to pull out a spreading patch of *Tibouchina,* look for more snails, and finally descend to the waiting vehicles. Then, slowly, we bounce our way back down the rutted road to McGregor Point. As we approach sea level, the heat comes back again. When we come to the chained fence, I get out of Bob's truck, unlock it, and let him drive through. Then, closing the fence behind him, I gaze back up at the West Maui mountains and notice, amidst the glimmering mists and gathering clouds, the faint hint of an emerging rainbow.

3

Eye of the Tiger

This is a true story, told to me by a local shark expert. A man, probably a tourist but maybe a local, is scuba diving in thirty feet of water off Maui. He is carefully working a piece of coral off a rock with a small hammer, something that he ought not to be doing in the first place. If he weren't quite so absorbed in removing the coral, he would notice that all of the little reef fish have suddenly ducked into their hidey-holes in the reef. He taps his way around the base of the coral and gently slips a pry bar underneath to pop it loose. Finally, he snaps the coral off its base, turns around—and finds himself nose-to-nose with a ten-foot shark.

Judging from the description—blunt snout, vertical bars on the sides, formidable size—the animal he confronted was a tiger shark *(Galeocerdo cuvieri)* that had followed the tapping sound to its source. As luck would have it, this particular encounter ended with a mutually satisfying withdrawal. Fish and human were jointly surprised and equally startled. It could have been different. Shark attacks occur in Hawai'i once a year

17

on average. All are frightening, a few are fatal, and tigers are usually implicated.

Of the 450 species of sharks that exist worldwide, forty occur in Hawaiian waters. They range in size from a true small fry—the eight-inch deep-water pygmy shark—to a genuine giant, the whale shark, which grows to forty-five feet and more and is the largest fish in the world. Other sharks are occasional visitors to Hawai'i, but it is the powerful and dangerous tiger shark that makes human adrenaline start to pump. And with good reason. Tiger sharks are the stuff of nightmares, huge, muscular creatures shaped like torpedoes and equipped with disproportionately large mouths and razor-sharp teeth. They can also be aggressive.

Consider surfer Rick Gruzinsky's brush with mortality. In October 1992 he paddled his surfboard out to a favorite shore break at a place called Laniākea on the island of O'ahu. About 150 yards from shore, the water under his board churned, bubbled, and then exploded up like a water fountain. Rick was catapulted into the air as a large shark chomped down on his board and bit out a two-foot semicircular section. Gruzinsky fought for control of his mangled board and made it back to shore without a scratch. Others haven't been so lucky.

Gruzinsky's confrontation may have been part of an un-usual pattern of attacks. Sightings of tiger sharks by ocean users have always been common in Hawai'i, but in the early 1990s, shark attacks inexplicably escalated. During one two-year period, two swimmers were killed and eight other body boarders, fishermen, and divers were attacked or bitten. Tiger sharks were also suspected in the disappearance of sev-eral surfers. After each attack, State-contracted shark hunters combed coastal waters and removed as many of the animals as they could find, almost always over the objections of biologists and *kanaka maoli.* The debate over tiger sharks continues to be acrimonious.

Indisputably, tiger sharks are one of the most fearsome creatures inhabiting equatorial waters. However, they were also revered by the people of Polynesia. And for good reason. Tigers, along with the great white shark, occupy the highest stratum of the marine food chain. They are massive and powerful animals that attain a length of eighteen feet. Most important, they strike fear, and sometimes panic, in human hearts whenever they show up. The old Hawaiian culture knew this fear also. In their pantheon, most sharks were treated as gods and considered to be the protectors of certain families. Some large man-eating sharks, however, were considered evil.

Was that ancient fear and its modern-day counterpart really justified? Opinions divide in interesting ways. "The conventional wisdom on tiger sharks," says Jerry Crowe, a researcher at the Waikīkī Aquarium, "is that they are indiscriminate eating machines that will snap up anything that comes their way." Although Crowe doesn't exactly see them this way, he acknowledges that scientists and fishermen do find an interesting assortment of things inside them. Usually, it is fish, lobsters, seals, and turtles, but examinations of tiger shark stomach contents have also revealed coconuts, horseshoes, license plates, ladies' handbags, and pieces of concrete.

Tiger sharks also have the annoying habit of showing up at the same places humans like to go. They cruise coastal reefs and patrol stream mouths after rain storms. In deeper water, they follow fishing boats looking for leftovers. Ordinary people usually experience a sense of terror when tigers come around, but close observers see their behavior as enigmatic. Jacques-Yves Cousteau found that tiger sharks would often disdain hooks baited with fresh beef. On the other hand, his crew once captured a ten-foot tiger shark that had eaten an entire side of beef that had gone bad and been tossed overboard from the *Calypso*. The rancid carcass had been wrapped in sackcloth and weighted with ballast. The shark ate everything.

If one side of the tiger shark argument is about human foreboding, the other side is pure statistics. Swimmers, surfers, fishermen, body boarders, and divers all seem to be vulnerable. On a pure numbers basis, however, tiger sharks just don't pose a significant danger. "In Hawai'i," says risk assessment specialist Kirk Smith, a former researcher at the East-West Center, "there is a far greater chance of getting run over by a motorboat or jet ski than bitten by a shark. Nonetheless," he says with a wry smile, "we all know that Hollywood will never make a movie called *Propeller.*"

Kim Holland, a zoologist and acknowledged tiger shark expert at the University of Hawai'i's Institute of Marine Biology, couldn't agree more. For the past five years he and a team of graduate students have been studying the movements of Hawai'i's tiger sharks to test the idea that their wholesale removal immediately after attacks have occurred improves public safety. Holland is skeptical of human shark policies and intrigued by the tigers themselves. He describes them as "mysterious, magnificent animals."

Holland is no armchair observer. His research is hands-on. Overnight, and just offshore of O'ahu's busiest beaches, Holland and his group will set out a longline with twenty to thirty five-inch hooks baited with old tuna heads. Each hook is on a thirty-foot leader. The next day, they will use a small skiff to check their lines. If they have caught a tiger shark, they will bring the tired animal up slowly, tow it to the main boat, secure a rope around the tail and head, and then roll the shark onto its back.

This maneuver tranquilizes the animal by inducing a state called "tonic immobility." Once the shark is on its back, Holland makes a small incision in the shark's belly and inserts an acoustic transmitter about the size of a large tube of sunscreen. He sews the shark up, releases it, and then tracks it by means of a series of listening posts that have been placed just offshore. By carefully monitoring each shark for several years, Holland can pinpoint exactly which sharks show up off O'ahu and with what frequency. In all, more than 150 tiger sharks, all over ten feet long, have been tagged and released off O'ahu.

And Holland's preliminary findings? He believes that tiger shark attacks are aberrant behavior. "It is amazing how many tigers are out there, how far they range, how finicky their eating habits are, and how rarely they bother anybody." Like other scientists, Holland used to believe that Hawai'i's tiger sharks populate a fairly small home range and simply patrolled individual territories. His bottom monitors, along with other data, have shown just the opposite. They travel extensively and move large distances in short periods of time. "The fish that is here right now will be on its way to Maui or the Penguin Banks off Moloka'i later today."

Holland, Crowe, and other researchers worry about other issues. "If we hunt out the large predators like tiger sharks," says Jerry Crowe, "we really don't know what the impact will be on other fish populations, including the ones that we value and rely on for food." Some scientists call this the "butterfly effect" in which small disturbances can have huge and some-times disastrous consequences. In a world of complex causes and effects, so the saying goes, it may just be the wing beat of a butterfly in Russia that causes thunderstorms over Florida and sunshine in Seattle.

Despite Holland's reassurances, human fear of sharks is not likely to be allayed any time soon. One day not so long ago, for example, a throng of people visiting Hanauma Bay suddenly deserted the park's shallow waters when someone reported that a large shark was cruising through the corals. Maybe it was an image of Gruzinsky fighting off a tiger shark or one too many fang-and-claw films on television. Whatever happened, several thousand people exited the water onto dry land in record time.

Hanauma Bay is one of the most popular underwater parks in the world. Each day people from 8 to 80 snorkel in and around the shallow reef gawking at fish and getting gawked at in return by beautiful sea creatures. On this particular day a swimmer who had stroked out about seventy-five yards suddenly came zipping back to shore to report his sighting. Word spread down the beach that a tiger shark was prowling around.

Divers, snorkelers, waders, and reef walkers beat a hasty retreat. One visitor from Japan who didn't quite understand what all the fuss was about had it explained to him through hand gestures by an accommodating American. "Ah," he said, watching someone imitate a fin carving through the water, "Jaw-zu!" As it turned out, the critter causing all the commotion was a docile three-and-a-half-foot white-tipped reef shark that was snoozing on a ledge just off the beach.

White-tipped reef sharks are completely harmless to humans. They sleep during the day and feed at night. In the course of a few hours, the shark signs that were posted (right next to the ones warning of waves, sunburn, and jellyfish) were taken down and reef visitations by humans returned to normal. In the end, the sleepy little critter took up residence at Hanauma for a few days and then wandered off in search of new people to scare.

4

Feed Willy

In Hawai'i—on any small island for that matter—all things are related. If they seem to be disconnected, it is just an illusion, a mere one-degree separation that will dissipate as soon as you probe the distinctions. Take the Kokubun clan, a family of former city people who twenty years ago intentionally chose to live their lives in the country. Apart from visits back to Honolulu to see family and friends, they have never looked back.

What keeps them where they are is a deep sense of connection. Precisely where Russell and Anne Kokubun call home is a small farm on the outer edge of a little town called Volcano, which is just across the highway from Hawai'i Volcanoes National Park. The land around them is volcanic, deep, craggy, filled with fire, and bubbling with geological vitality. In the community of Volcano, these ancient lavas are carpeted by rain forest, and in the midst of that forest, there are pastures and farms. One of those four-acre spreads belongs to the Kokubuns.

In addition to growing artichokes, zucchinis, and snapdragons for the Hilo and Honolulu markets, Russell is the former head of the Hawai'i County Council, a former director of the Hilo Main Street Program, and recently appointed to the State Senate. His wife Anne is a veteran special education teacher. Although Russell and Anne hail originally from Honolulu and Pittsburgh, respectively, their two girls have grown up on the Big Island. Nina goes to the local high school. Keiko is a freshman at the University of Hawai'i in Hilo. Then there is Willy. "Willy-Boy," as he is currently called, is also a member of the Kokubun clan, but Willy-Boy has a few problems.

First, there's his weight. Girth-wise, all the rest of the Kokubuns are pretty normal in size. Willy is 350 pounds, and climbing. His attitude is also an issue. Although he retains the sweet, sunny outlook of Kokubuns everywhere, Willy-Boy has a few teenage punk tendencies that sometimes get him in trouble. Like running around late at night. Like hamming it up and nudging and begging for food. Like putting his head down, exploding straight at you at sixty miles an hour, and then stopping just short of sudden impact and staring at you with soft, innocent eyes and a Beavis and Butthead look that says: "Just kidding . . . heh heh."

Most of all, Willy has what now appears to be a permanent identity crisis. He thinks he is human. And despite his four legs, bristly hide, curving tusks, probing snout, and curlicue tail, the Kokubuns suspect he may be right.

Willy, you see, is a wild Hawaiian boar, a member of that famous—and to some people, infamous—species whose dual origins trace back to the landing of the first Polynesian canoes somewhere around A.D. 500 and the arrival of Captain James Cook's ship in 1778. Pigs hold a distinguished place in human history. From the African warthog to the English boar, they seem to have been with us always. They are the stuff of literature (George Orwell's *Animal Farm*), of poetry (Thomas Hood's "The Lament of Toby"), and of fortune-telling (The Chinese Horoscope). Most of all, they are food—ham, bacon, cutlets, ham hocks, pork loins, and pickled pig's feet.

In Hawai'i they are also special. Today's Hawaiian pig, a blend of Polynesian and European strains, can be found almost anywhere, including my neighborhood in urban Honolulu. One of them once scared the bejesus out of my kids when they saw one looking in the window down in our basement. They are also a source of controversy. Scientists attribute the preponderance of the damage to Hawai'i's native plants and birds to introduced species. Pigs, they say, are the worst offenders because they are prolific breeders and indiscriminate rooters.

The other side of the coin are local hunters, many of whom are *kanaka maoli*. They see pigs as an esteemed cultural resource. Pigs figure prominently in the legends of ancient deities that children still hear at home. In pre-Contact times, pigs were sometimes breast-fed by women and closely managed in Hawaiian households, just like Willy. Wild pigs, however, became food. They were—and still are—hunted by *kanaka maoli* men and their dogs, most often with guns, but sometimes in the more traditional way with knives and spears. These hog battles are a matter of ritual, honor, and pride.

Between pest and produce, however, lies a third possibility. According to a few people, the Hawaiian pig—a notably oversized, irritable, and uncivilized critter—can also be a pet. Enter Willy-Boy.

One day Russell was visiting his old friend Michael Gomes, who lives on the other side of the island. Mike had a couple of wild shoats that had been orphaned and one of them, the one named "Piggy-Girl," eventually broke out for a night of carousing. The result was a litter of her own. Mike offered one of Piggy-Girl's progeny to Russell, who being a former city kid, had always wanted one, and the great Kokubun study on the inner lives of wild piglets was under way.

Russell trundled Willy home in his van and introduced the baby porker to Anne, Keiko, and Nina. For Keiko and Nina, it was love at first sight. The kids named him Wilbur (of *Charlotte's Web* fame), built a small pen, transformed an old doghouse into a pig house, and commenced feeding, washing, and loving him as if he were a new brother. In short order, Wilbur's very human and somewhat extroverted personality started to emerge.

"I was surprised at how he much he resembled a puppy," says Anne. "He would play tug of war with a stick or cloth. He would hide in his box and then coyly peep at people from around the corner. Every once in a while he would escape from the pen, race around the yard, visit the neighbor's horse and make a ruckus, force Keiko and Nina to chase him, and then, when he was tired, return to his pen."

In the end, however, it was Russell and Anne who became the primary caregivers. On a steady menu of grain, sweet potatoes, and kitchen scraps, Wilbur started to grow. "When he got to be about a hundred pounds," says Russell, "his name sort of changed to Willy. When he got to be two hundred pounds, he became Willy-Boy." Food, of course, was a great motivator. If you are a pig, says Russell Kokubun authoritatively, food is an all-consuming business. That's why Willy loves old frosting from the refrigerator, leftover fish, watermelon rinds, grubs, slugs, and the pits from peaches, plums, and bing cherries, which he crunches down like hard candy.

On a Sunday afternoon with sunlight streaming down from a crystal-blue sky and trade winds blowing through the apple trees that ring the Kokubun farm, I pay a visit to see how Willy-Boy is doing. Russell and Anne are moving the pen, which they do periodically to rototill sections of their garden. They clean the water dish, rewire portions of the fence, hose down the dog/pig house, fix up a new wallow, scratch him behind his ears, and keep up a steady conversation with him.

Willy noses around his now rearranged front yard, then slowly saunters over to Russell, who pulls a large can out of a bag. Willy-Boy looks up expectantly and then every one of his 350 pounds starts to vibrate with excitement. Whipped cream, preferably in the family-sized can and blasted directly into his mouth by the loving hands of Russell or Anne, is Willy-Boy's absolute favorite food. "Sit, Willy!" Russell commands. Willy-Boy lowers himself down on his haunches and opens his mouth. In goes sixteen high-pressure ounces of thick, rich, white whipped cream.

From a porcine point of view, no less than a human one, it is apparent that this low-maintenance pig experiment run by the Kokubuns is Nirvana. Through some luck of the cosmic draw, Willy has stumbled directly into hog heaven: plenty of food, hanging out with nice people, no hunters, low rent. Fat as a baby rhinoceros, tail swishing, he keeps up a steady stream of barely audible grunts, chirps, barks, and squeaks, all of which are the Willy-Boy equivalent of saying "Hey, this is great. I'm OK, you're OK, and life is OK. Just keep feeding me more whipped cream."

And Willy-Boy's future? Everybody who comes to visit wants to know when the Kokubuns plan on turning Willy-Boy into bacon and pork chops. "They measure him out in the number of sausages that could get made," says Russell. Luckily for Willy, such is not to be. For the Kokubuns, Willy-Boy is one of those bonds that typify life on an island where all lives, including pig lives and human lives, ultimately intertwine in ways that no one could ever have predicted. It is that kind of connection that Russell and Anne sought when they moved to the country. It's what Willy has helped them find.

5

Small Perfections

Viewed from a certain narrow angle, the daily round in Honolulu is like life in any other medium-sized city. On my desk, at that specific intersection where cup-of-pencils meets in-tray-exploding-with-papers, I have a framed cartoon that I look at every day for courage. It shows a beleaguered guy in his office answering his telephone with: "No, Thursday's out. How about never. Does never work for you?"

Even in gracious, easygoing Hawai'i, things get complicated. Call it "Rat Race in Paradise." Work is filled with meetings, deadlines, and a small Sierra Nevada of overdue correspondence. The home front has its own chaos: sixth-grade homework assignments you can't understand, the broken door hinge that defies all conventional fixes, an overdue root canal, and a prolonged visit from two long-lost aunties who have come to Hawai'i to stay for a week, or maybe two, or maybe forever.

Sound familiar? For just a moment, take a deep breath, shoo away all those mental ducks that are pecking at your fingers

29

and toes, let your body relax, and imagine a different sort of universe that is smaller and quieter. In this encapsulated far-away cosmos, time slows down and sometimes stops altogether. Looking around, you see the abiding forms of stone, earth, sky, and water. You soak in these basal elements and for an instant you experience something that approaches that most precious of contemporary commodities: tranquility.

Nearly every community has one or two places that offer this kind of respite: the local park, the nearby forest or lake, that special hilltop where people go to get away from it all. Hawai'i has many such places, usually smaller in scale, but always filled with surprises that reflect the interplay of Eastern, Western, and Oceanic cultures and island landscapes. Some take an hour to reach and require expeditionary preparations. Others, however, are right around the corner.

On a Sunday morning my 11-year-old daughter Kelly and I zip out of the driveway on bikes and head due east. Bike riding is something Kelly discovered a few years ago after a prolonged parent-child standoff. Eyes flashing, feet stamping, mouth formed into a major pout, she declared: "I have to have training wheels." Cool as ice, I said: "Completely unnecessary." Back and forth. Finally, we compromised. "If you aren't up and running in fifteen minutes," I told her, "I buy you training wheels." It took her seven minutes, several long smears of bicycle grease, and one slightly skinned knee to become a total bike fiend.

So, today, we are off. Our destination is the campus of the University of Hawai'i and the shaded Japanese garden that sits behind the East-West Center. Both institutions are less than a mile from our house and a simple cruise through our tree-lined neighborhood. For myself, I am after some of that composure and serenity that is supposed to emanate from beautiful gardens and a little father-daughter bonding time.

Kelly is interested in bike riding and any general adventures that might present themselves on the way.

This particular garden is the 1963 endowment of Japanese benefactors and a group of landscape architects from Asia, the Pacific, and the United States. Its central feature is a small, carefully sculpted waterway that has been diverted from the much larger, longer, and free-flowing Mānoa Stream. Like the rest of the garden, the elaborately constructed watercourse is laden with symbolism.

Just as a river begins in the high mountains, broadens through the plains, and slows as it reaches the sea, the channeled waters of this specific garden roll over a small waterfall, wander past a Japanese teahouse, and then fall into a pond filled with lovely, fat orange and red carp. These three physical levels of what is by any measure just a small babbling brook parallel the three ages all of us pass through: the turmoil and energy of youth, the steadiness and productivity of adulthood, the dignity and perspective of old age.

We park the bikes, enter the garden, and follow the meandering gravel pathway down to the koi pond. In this carefully contoured world, the carp live a prosperous and well-fed life. Dozens of unusual plantings—some traditional, some contemporary, some local, some imported—surround them. We wander through strawberry guava and Surinam cherry, Japanese hibiscus and mock orange, cinnamon and jasmine, juniper and pine, gardenia and weeping willow, and—dominating everything on a small knoll—a pink cassia tree planted by Prince Akihito and Princess Michiko of Japan during a visit in 1964.

Gray stone lanterns and mustard-colored bamboo dot the grounds of the garden. Below the teahouse that was built by Mr. Soshitsu Sen, a fifteenth-generation Grand Tea Master of Urasenke Konnichian, we settle ourselves on some flat rocks. Kelly pokes a finger in the water, wiggles it around, and a dozen curious koi swim toward her. For a time, we simply sit and watch the fish slowly finning through the water. I am wondering if their little world is really as calm as it looks.

Eventually, we wander over to the garden's eastern edge, look around, jump a fence, drop down a six-foot embankment, and enter the jumbled forest world of Mānoa Stream itself. Very few of the thousands of visitors who come to this garden each year actually see the stream because it is hidden from view by a large berm. Yet, here, on the banks of this small, narrow river descending from Oʻahu's central mountain range, on a little path maintained by a few hiking enthusiasts, nature presents a completely different face.

Sunlight slants through a canopy of overhanging trees. Some parts of the stream are suffused in a soft yellow light illuminating clouds of gnats swimming through the air. Other places are cast into deep shadow. The wet edges of the stream are lined with grasses and creaking trees. White butterflies flutter along the banks and a Shama Thrush darts through the underbrush. The other residents of this wet, muddy world are small fish, mosquitoes, spiders, frogs, tadpoles, and dragon-flies with large, translucent wings.

While I am inspecting the swirling eddy of a rock, Kelly picks up a stick, doodles in the dried mud, and then calls me over to examine three large, green insects she has discovered. For all of its refinement and symbolism, the cloistered little Japanese garden above is missing certain things. Big, green bugs, for example. "Do you like it here?" I ask Kelly. "It's cleaner in the garden," she answers, "but there's more things to see and touch down here."

A perfect summation, I think to myself. East meets West. The garden and the bush: two kinds of tranquility, two kinds of nature, two kinds of perfection. Not better, not worse, just different. One is manicured, one is wild. One is cleaned and trimmed daily by gardeners. The other is more or less abandoned and left to its own Darwinian ways.

On the other side of the stream we pick up a trail and follow it downstream past several little waterfalls. We amble along not quite knowing where we are going. As it turns out, the path leads to a third perfection.

At a little bend in the stream, Native Hawaiian students from the University of Hawai'i have constructed a small dam and, behind it, they have restored a narrow aqueduct channeling water half a mile onto a tract of land called "Kua Pāpā Lo'i O Kānewai," meaning "row of taro patches near the spring of Kāne's healing waters." This particular plot of land brings together the basic, everyday plants nurtured by ancient *kanaka maoli*. It is run by and for Hawaiian students, who have spent many a weekend rebuilding the old ditches and bunds.

The workshed where students and visitors usually congregate is empty. We take the liberty of walking through the two and a half acres of streamside land that are under cultivation. We see little parcels of sugarcane, sweet potatoes, and yams. Trees that were important in the daily lives of ancient Hawaiians—pandanus, candlenut, coconut, breadfruit, and paper mulberry—have been planted on the perimeter to produce fruits and serve as shade and windbreaks. The center of the garden is made up of taro patches, all carefully irrigated by the little ditch that starts upstream by the pond.

Taro, a plant found throughout Polynesia, was a staple part of the Hawaiian diet and a revered and central aspect of Hawaiian mythology. These particular taro lands, I learn later, belonged to Hawaiian royalty and were in a continuous and high state of cultivation centuries before Captain Cook steered the *Resolution* into Hawaiian waters. Today, they are a quiet and unspoken symbol of cultural persistence.

Juxtaposed with the spare elegance of the Japanese garden and the lush beauty of Mānoa Stream's wild banks, Kua Pāpā

Loʻi O Kānewai offers a living celebration of the agricultural adaptations of the first people to come to these Islands. It is another kind of Eden. But paradise, as we all know in our heart-of-hearts, isn't really a place. It's a state of mind, a small and momentary perfection, that we sometimes find hidden amidst the ebb, flow, and flotsam of daily life.

Enveloped by the luminous beauties of these three different streamside environments, we head back up the path to our bikes. Kelly walks next to me, humming a Hawaiian melody and holding my hand. In the foot-after-foot rhythm of the walking I notice the patches of taro, the leafy path, the spreading forest, the clipped hedges of the garden, Kelly, and all the other quintessential shapes and forms of Mānoa Stream; deep in the marrow of my being, I know that all of these things are fundamentally connected and in a state that, for lack of any better language, we sometimes call grace.

6

Unsolved Murder

7:30 A.M., Saturday morning. Close to the 7,000-foot level of the highest mountain in Hawai'i: Mauna Kea. This really is our lucky day. We shouldn't be here, but we have managed to escape undetected. Nonetheless, there is a certain element of guilt and a mutual recognition of dangers on the home front. If Russell and I were mature, stable adults who acted our age we would renounce weekend wandering and head back to our respective homes to do more of those chores that keep the respective home fires burning. Russ would be planting sweet potatoes on his farm in Volcano. I would be mowing a thick, weed-choked, vine-infested backyard in Honolulu that is slowly reverting to its island rain forest origins.

But all of these obligations must wait. Adventure has called and Russell Kokubun and I have responded like a couple of Pavlov's dogs sitting in front of a large meatball. Following up on the barest wisp of a story heard from a biologist at the University of Hawai'i, we are hunting for a little dot on a topographic map called "Kaluakauka," literally "the pit of the doctor." More specifically, this trip is all about finding a certain stone marker that, if it still exists, stands on the exact spot where one of the world's greatest botanists was killed in 1834 under circumstances that to this day remain confused, enigmatic, and a topic of debate among historians.

The man's name was David Douglas and his main legacy and namesake is *Pseudotsuga menziesii*. This is the same plant we see when we rummage around in lumberyards looking for a straight two-by-four or when it is time to find a well-proportioned tree to put up at Christmas: the Douglas Fir. Douglas, it turns out, was an indefatigable traveler and collector who cataloged thousands of new plants and animals and singlehandedly introduced more than 150 new trees and shrubs into England. It is also a little-known fact that he met his untimely end in the Hawaiian Islands not far from where we are now ricocheting down a dusty dirt road on the flanks of Mauna Kea in Russell's white pickup truck.

Free of the city and pinging off the ruts, rocks, and washboards, the adventure is off to a splendid start. Russell and I are in fine fettle and full of conversation about friends, family, and the task before us. I am clucking away about how clever we are to have escaped today's householding duties and Russell is regaling me with stories of unfinished tasks, including cleaning Willy-Boy's pigpen and apologizing to the neighbors for Willy's latest harassment of their horses. "He thinks those horses are pigs," Russell explains with a look of resignation. My sympathies are with him as I offer him various policy options: (a) build a $5,000 steel and concrete pigpen; (b) rent him to the neighbors as a horse-guarding watch pig; or (c) buy Willy his own horse.

It is also a stunningly glorious morning. We are blessed with clear skies, brilliant sunshine, and crisp mountain air. The landscape we are driving over is lunar. It is filled with massive, angular formations—old tuff and cinder cones and hundreds of smaller red, brown, ocher, and rust-colored rocks that were shot out and strewn about the mountain several centuries ago. On top of everything else, there is a cooler full of sandwiches, several cans of beer, and a couple of fat cigars just waiting to be pulled out in the shade of the right tree—a Douglas Fir if we can find one.

In this sublime and less-visited region of Hawai'i, there are also many other interesting natural objects that bear noting. Grasses and shrubs interest Russell. There is wild raspberry, *'ōhelo* with its bright red edible berries, and a long stretch of flowering gorse that has its origins in Scotland. We stop to inspect the yellow flowers and thorns of this intrusive pest, and Russell reminds me that plants and the British Isles are central to the Douglas story.

Born of common means in a time of rigid class distinctions in Perthshire, Scotland, Douglas was apprenticed at age 11 as a gardener's assistant at the palace of the Earl of Mansfield. By dint of sheer intelligence and stamina and a wild curiosity about the natural world, he rose quickly. At 24 he was appointed botanical collector to what is now England's Royal Horticultural Society, and, in that capacity, he became the first botanist to systematically explore the flora and fauna of California, Oregon, Washington, and Hawai'i.

In 1823 he made his way to the Oregon Territory and over the next decade traveled extensively throughout the American and Canadian West. Douglas roamed as far north as Hudson Bay and then south along the Cascade and Sierra Nevada Ranges. A prodigious walker, it is estimated that he covered nearly 12,000 miles by foot, horse, and canoe, discovering, in the course of these travels, seventeen different pine and spruce trees, dozens of poppies and lupines, and the only peony found in the Western Hemisphere.

But Douglas was more than a scientist. On his journeys west, and on the road to his final resting spot in Hawai'i, he confronted grizzly bears and arrows; shot the rapids of the Columbia River; clambered up the highest peaks in the Rockies; came close to death by drowning, frostbite, and infection; and fell in love with a Chinook Indian princess. Throughout these experiences he continuously and persistently sought out new animals and plants, kept detailed scientific journals, and shipped specimens back to what was then the premier horticultural society in the world.

But there were problems, especially toward the end. Late in 1833, after a frustrating and disappointing expedition to British Columbia, he boarded a schooner bound for the Hawaiian Islands and, after a brief stay with the British consul in Honolulu, spent several months exploring the island of Hawai'i. He climbed the summits of Mauna Kea and Mauna Loa, camped at Kīlauea Volcano, and, in a frenzy of collecting, cataloged hundreds of new plants. He then returned to Honolulu to ship his specimens home and deal with various personal matters.

Tired, restless, and financially pressed, Douglas then set off on a coastal steamer bound back to Hilo on the Big Island. He never reached his destination. Instead, he disembarked at 'Upolu Point in Kohala with his favorite dog, determined to walk across Mauna Kea on an overland trail and avoid the hard weather that was slowing the ship's progress. His path—the same road we are now driving in Russell's pickup truck—led him into the rain forest and the wild world of Hawai'i's cattle hunters. These rugged men made their livings trapping stray animals in large, camouflaged pits.

Douglas spent what would be his last night in the hut of one of these mountain men, an Englishman and former convict from Botany Bay named Edward Gurney. Gurney seems to have warned Douglas about the dangers of the cattle pits that dotted the higher elevations of Mauna Kea at the time. Nonetheless, the next day Douglas set off at a brisk pace to cover the forty miles remaining to Hilo. His frame of mind, speculated biographer William Morwood in *Traveler in a Vanished Landscape* published in 1973, was decidedly down. "He had alienated old friends by boasts and insults, and alarmed new ones by a garrulity he seemed unable to control. He, who had once been celebrated along the Columbia River for his tact and patience with Indians, had taken to abusing Hawaiian guides and baggage carriers to the extent that none would work for him twice."

Later that same day, Douglas was discovered at the bottom of one of the cattle traps. The agitated bull that was in the pit with him was killed by some of Gurney's men and Douglas' body was retrieved and conveyed to Hilo. There, after inspection by another cattle hunter and the noting of certain peculiar head wounds, the first suggestions of foul play were raised. Those suspicions have never been fully allayed.

Jostling our way over the bumpy road girdling Mauna Kea, we pass the Hakalau Wildlife Refuge and the corrals and cattle chutes of several ranches. Eventually, we come to the spot marked Kaluakauka on our topographic map. We park the truck, lace our boots, and head into the dense foliage that surrounds us. Following the remains of an old path, Russell clears overhanging vines with a machete. We work our way in half a mile. It is hot, sweaty work and it is painfully obvious that no visitors have been here recently. Inevitably, the path disappears into a maze of wild pig trails and a tangle of chest-high grass and underbrush.

Finally, after much searching, we stumble into a small clearing and find the David Douglas memorial. Truthfully speaking, we are completely unprepared for the size and beauty of the monument. It is nearly eight feet tall and rests on a raised concrete platform. It is pyramidal in shape and constructed of dark and stately basaltic stones that must have been brought in at great time and expense by horseback. In the middle of the monument sits a brass plate that reads as follows:

KALUAKAUKA
In Memory of
D^r. David Douglas

Killed Near This Spot
In A Wild Bullock Pit

July 12, 1834 A.D.

A small plaque on the other side notes the memorial's construction by a group of distinguished foresters and botanists who dedicated it on July 12, 1934. The monument is ringed by towering Douglas Firs planted six decades ago.

Sitting quietly at this nearly forgotten memorial, it is impossible not to ruminate on the life and times of an intrepid explorer. Eclipsed by the breakneck pace of today's technological and social changes, Douglas' journeys of the early nineteenth century seem less important than the current quest to decode DNA, calibrate global warming, or put a space station into permanent high orbit. Nonetheless, a quiet tribute to his accomplishments persists both at the memorial and in the community of scholars and scientists who study natural history. Douglas (who heroically shunned all forms of lawn mowing and pumpkin planting) has more plants named after him than any other botanist.

But the mystery surrounding his death also abides. Was he really murdered? The money Douglas was rumored to be carrying the day he died was never found and it is clear from where his dog and rucksack were discovered that he had actually doubled back—or was enticed to return—to the pit where he was found. Nothing could be proved, however. A few days after his death, Douglas' body was sent to Honolulu for burial in an unmarked grave at Kawaiha'o Church. He was 35 years old.

As for the cattle catchers of Mauna Kea, no charges were ever brought against Gurney or his men. Gurney disappeared into the California Gold Rush a few years later and was never heard from again. Rumors of a deathbed confession implicating a Hawaiian cowboy floated among some Big Island families for a time, but sorting out the essential truth of fading memories was, and always is, a precarious business.

As with so many other legends that circulate on a small, far-flung island in the middle of the Pacific, nobody knows what really happened or, if they do, they simply won't tell. Secrets are an island way, of course. Hard as they may be to keep in small and intimate places, some of them persist forever.

Fish Central

The deep, cool waters that surround the 1,500-mile length of the Hawaiian Islands are blessed with a wonderful array of sea life. There are great varieties of fish, both nearshore and pelagic. There are lobsters and crabs. There are limpets, urchins, eels, and all manner of creatures that swim, stump, wiggle, walk, or shoot through Hawai'i's azure waters. For those with taste buds that hanker after seafood, many of these are wonderfully and deliciously edible.

Each night, much of this fare comes ashore in a variety of tubs, bins, and crates. Some of it is destined to be shipped out to points east or west, but much of what is caught is for local plates.

Seafood is a quietly thriving Hawaiian commerce. And it is something more. At local mom-and-pop stores and in hundreds of restaurants like Ethels Grill, the Drop Inn, and Danny's

43

Broiler, seafood brings out our Pacific, Asian, and North American heritages and helps create a common cultural denominator. It's a fact. Local people love to talk about, catch, cook, eat, or otherwise fiddle around with fish.

Premium fish is also central to the revolution that has recently swept through Island cookery. Culinary wizards like Beverly Gannon and Roy Yamaguchi (to name just two) have become famous for their "East Meets West" creations. Take sashimi, the raw, sliced tuna that is eaten in sushi bars with a little bit of Japanese horseradish. At her restaurant on Maui, Beverly Gannon uses large, dinner-size pieces, sears them with gourmet blackening spices, and serves them up with Thai chili sauce and local sweet potatoes. Roy Yamaguchi, on the other hand, will find himself a good chunk of fresh-caught dorado, cook it with red wine sauce, and present it with goat cheese hash, local vegetables, and maybe some papaya relish.

Cooking fusions like these are the end stage of a long process. From fin to fork and sea to soup, fish first pass through many other skilled hands, many of whom gather at the United Fishing Agency each morning when the rest of us are asleep. The United Fishing Agency is one of the last authentic fish auctions in the United States. It is a place where famous chefs and unknown fishmongers do business side-by-side. It is also a window into the heart of Hawai'i's amalgam of cultures.

To the unassuming, the Agency is just a large, dank building in Kaka'ako, the industrial part of Honolulu. To those in the know, it is something more akin to "fish central," the nerve center of a complex industry that involves thousands of people and some very big stakes. Fishing is a high-risk, high-gain enterprise. It has its own language and its own "rules of the road," which combine the vagaries of the marketplace with the vicissitudes of the sea. And like a well-run airport, the agency is a hub. Things converge, get sorted, get stacked, and are then dispersed to other destinations. It all starts around midnight when the first long-liners and trolling boats start off-loading their fish and bringing them to the Agency. At exactly 5:30 A.M., the commercial action picks up. A bell rings, the doors pop open, and a small crowd of wholesalers, peddlers, and retailers move into a large, chilly room with a concrete floor.

Inside, on pallets laid out in rows, are a rainbow of local fishes ranging in weight from two to 250 pounds and in shape from torpedolike to something that can only be described as blimpoid. In the middle of the floor, a knot of men and women crowd around the auctioneers. Wayne Higashi, a former political science major from the University of Hawai'i, and Brooks Takenaka, a marine biologist and third-generation fisherman, have been auctioning for the fish agency for more than a decade.

On the particular day I visit, Higashi works his way down a long row of pallets while workers in gum boots and old army jackets scuttle by with trolleys filled with more fish. Most of the fish being sold are known by their Japanese or Hawaiian names. There are long, skinny wahoo *(ono)*, Pacific blue marlin *(kajiki)*, striped marlin *(nairagi)*, dorado *(mahimahi)*, bigscale pomfret *(monchong)*, moonfish *(opah)*, groupers *(hāpu'upu'u)*, broadbill swordfish *(shutome)*, and shortbill spearfish *(hebi)*.

Although everything has its own season, the most prized fishes right now are the tunas, especially the "big eye" *('ahi)* and the yellowfin *(shibi)*. Tuna buyers, many from Hawai'i's larger and better-known markets and restaurants, inspect their fish carefully before bidding. As the buyers look the fish over, they will stick a couple of fingers inside a clean, transverse cut near the tail, grab some flesh, pull it out, sniff it, and rub it in their hands. They are checking for color, texture, and fat content. Two *'ahi* that look exactly the same on the outside can be completely different inside. One will sell for $1.20 a pound. The one next to it will go for $5.50.

As the purchased fish are carted off, new ones are brought in. Higashi moves to a new row and the buyers follow. He waggles a finger, fires off a string of numbers, points again, and two of the blimpy, red and gray moonfish with white spots, each weighing 110 pounds, are sold for $1.50 a pound. Moments later, a dozen *mahimahi* in the twenty-five-pound range, their oddly oversized heads and green-brown bodies gleaming, are sold off along with a pile of pink snappers, known locally as *'ōpakapaka.* A cart with ten-pound *onagas,* or ruby snappers, is brought in and unloaded. They get sold along with a dozen striped marlin.

Standing in the midst of so much seafood, I am transfixed by the interplay of fish and human and the complicated signals being telegraphed back and forth by buyers and auctioneer. The fish move in, Higashi points and mumbles, the buyers look and twitch, the purchase gets made, the fish move out. But there is other activity as well. People are coordinating with shippers by cellular phone, weighing the large midsections of mako sharks, and supervising the comings and goings of various trucks. Some of what heads out the door will end up in the upscale eateries that Chefs Yamaguchi and Gannon have made famous. Some will also end up in a bucket of fish heads sold for chowder in Chinatown.

Amidst all this hurly-burly, a worker wearing baggy flower shorts and black tennis shoes pushes a cart down the aisle and scolds me for getting in the way. Mr. Frank Goto, the Agency's stoic general manager, stands on a staircase leading to the Agency's upstairs offices. He looks at me, nods, and continues to sweep a mindful and supervisory gaze over everything that is going on at the auction. He may also be doing some mental calculations like I'm trying to do. The United Fishing Agency takes 10 percent of everything that is sold. On a good day, 120,000 pounds of fish will move through the auction at anywhere from one dollar to ten dollars a pound. Today looks like a pretty good day.

One of this morning's buyers is a soft-spoken, hard-working regular named Don Leong. Don is in his late 40s. Born in China and raised in Honolulu, he still carries the faint lilt of a Chinese accent. Don, his wife Elaine, and his son Calvin own the Wing Sing Seafood Company, which buys, cleans, and distributes fish to some of Honolulu's best restaurants. The Leongs have their own small, spotlessly clean processing facility about three miles from the Agency. Don employs five people. Wearing yellow rubber aprons and wielding razor-sharp knives, any one of them can gut, trim, skin, bone, or fillet a fifteen-pound *onaga* in under three minutes.

Right now, Don has his eye on several prime pieces of fish including one especially plump and glistening *'ahi* fresh caught by the *Pacific Dream,* an eighty-five-foot long-liner. The *Pacific Dream* is part of a flotilla of some 175 boats that are permitted and homeported in Hawai'i. Once dominated by Japanese, most of the folks who now ply the local fleet are Korean and Vietnamese. *Pacific Dream,* however, is one of seven long-liners owned or managed by two local Caucasians named Sean Martin and Jim Cook.

Like the auction itself, a modern long-liner is a study in complexity and risk. Typical boats cost $750,000, carry a crew of four, range fifteen hundred miles from the Islands, and will stay at sea from twelve to eighteen days. While she is out there, a long-liner like *Pacific Dream* will repeatedly lay out a thirty- to forty-mile length of heavy monofilament line equipped with expensive radio beacons and upwards of 1,800 mackerel- or squid-baited hooks. On a good trip, owner and crew may catch $60,000 worth of swordfish and tuna. On a bad trip they get skunked and make nothing. On a really terrible trip, engines explode, typhoons come up, and boats sink.

At the auction, Don pushes his way into the cluster of buyers. He wags his fingers back and forth at Higashi, the auctioneer, who is playing him off another buyer. He wins the bid and slaps a Wing Sing Seafood Company tag on the *'ahi* he has just purchased for $2.60 a pound. It is now 7:45 A.M. An hour later the *'ahi,* along with the many other fish he has purchased, are trucked to the Wing Sing warehouse. Quickly, carefully, the fish are cleaned, packaged, and chilled.

In midmorning, and then again in the late afternoon, one of Don's trucks will make a run to the hotels he is selling fish to for today's lunch and dinner trade. One of the restaurants on his list is La Mer, Hawai'i's highly acclaimed, five-diamond restaurant at the ever-elegant Halekūlani Hotel. Don drops off nearly 400 pounds of fresh fish at the Halekūlani, some of which is for Chef de Cuisine Yves Garnier. Garnier is a tall and effusive Frenchman who cooks in an accomplished neoclassic style evolved from his many years in Monte Carlo and Provence. That Southern French influence, coupled with the sometimes unique and always fresh Hawaiian ingredients, produces what he calls a "cuisine of the sun."

Getting ready for his dinner guests in the late afternoon, Chef Garnier carefully supervises the kitchen staff who are starting to make culinary magic with the big eye, broadbill, snapper, moonfish, and wahoo. Tables are set, wines are decanted, and Chef Garnier fusses, twiggles, tweaks, and tastes. Then magic begins.

The broadbill caught by Martin and Cook's *Pacific Dream,* auctioned by Brooks Takenaka, filleted by Don Leong, and cooked by Yves Garnier becomes "Fillet of Shutome Crusted with Pancetta," a delicious mingling of firm white fish, smoky Italian bacon, and braised green cabbage. The ruby snappers turn into "Hawaiian Salt Crusted Onaga." They are served up with "Confit Tomato with Truffle Juice and Fried Basil." The big eye tuna is also transmogrified. It becomes *"Ahi* Tartar and Caviar." The choicest, raw, *sashimi*-quality tuna is minced, topped with Russian sturgeon eggs, placed on a small piece of toast, and served with a lemon-mustard sauce.

In the evening, with Waikīkī's waves lapping gently on the beach and an onshore breeze blowing through the open windows, it all comes together. Guests filter into La Mer's quiet interior for dinner. An elderly gentleman who lives in Hilo has come here to dine with his son and daughter-in-law. Two businessmen, one from New York, the other from Tokyo, are concluding an important transaction. A husband and wife are celebrating their twenty-fifth wedding anniversary.

Somewhere toward midnight, after the dessert and coffee have been served, after the dishes have been cleared, after the last guest has left and the last counter has been wiped, the lights at La Mer will slowly blink out. But for others just a few miles away, the work day is starting. The *Princess K,* a long-liner, is unloading at Pier 35. And down at the United Fishing Agency, the lights are going on and the first load of swordfish is being unloaded and weighed in.

Golfing through
El Niño

Compared with life in other latitudes, Hawai'i has it easy when it comes to weather. Nine out of ten days it's "Sunny, wind from the east 15 to 25 mph, mid-80s, some high clouds, and a few passing windward showers." On those rare days when things change, the temperature may tick up or down a few degrees, a swell might roll in (making the surfers happy), or a cold front may create a shear line that hovers just north of the Islands for a couple of days.

Aberrations do occur, however, and one of them is taking place now. A formidable chain of squalls is blowing over the central Pacific bringing high winds, cool temperatures, and drenching rains to the Islands. Outside my window, the streets are slick from thundershowers. Mānoa Valley, the mountain-ringed place we live in, is dark and vaporous. A thick curtain of mist is suspended across the mountains. Humidity and waterlogged air is today's real weather report.

Logically, this should be a morning to stay home and read spy novels or, if you must, to hole up in the office and attack piles of paper. But today, it is neither. Something truly demented is afoot. Two of my cronies, Neal Milner and Kem Lowry, have chosen this particular day to introduce me to a new sport: golf—something I swore I would never fool with until I was incapable of doing anything else. But golf, my buds have been telling me, is an important matter. It is a manly game over which big business deals get done and therefore an important part of being a grownup. Others disagree. "A Good Walk Ruined," is how one writer described it.

So the two of them swing by the house at a quarter past five in the morning wearing hats, T-shirts, shorts, and beat-up running shoes. I would prefer to ease into all this prearranged fun with a bit of discussion and a cup of coffee, but Neal says "Good morning," grabs my borrowed clubs, shoves me into the car, and off we go. As it turns out, the two of them, both full professors at the University of Hawai'i, are taking me to a public golf course located on a remote strand of beachfront near the town of Kahuku.

Kahuku is about as far away from Honolulu as you can get and still be on this island. It lies on the tip of O'ahu and sticks out into the ocean as if it was trying to escape from the rest of the island. On a normal day, Kahuku is windy. Today, it will be fierce. Undeterred, my two pals are primed for action. "We have to get there early," says Kem as I stare into the escalating monsoon, "otherwise the other golfers may see us."

Neal and Kem are not regulars. They do not even qualify as irregulars. They play exactly once each year. The annual match is a pilgrimage of sorts, a rite of passage in which the two of them sneak away from campus and spend the day goofing off. "Pondering philosophical matters and high-level policy concerns," explains Neal, "that's what we are doing." "We need to mull and cogitate about the really big picture," adds Kem. For years they have been offering to take me along and teach me the game. This year, counterintuitive though it be, I have succumbed.

As we drive over the Ko'olau Mountains, the radio gives us the first weather report of the day. Expect high winds, fierce rains, and hazardous driving conditions, says the newscaster. It is all part of El Niño, he goes on to explain, that much-maligned thermal anomaly that is causing atmospheric and oceanographic changes around the globe. El Niño is responsible for snow in Africa, sunshine in England, mud slides in California, cold fronts in Mexico, forest fires in Indonesia, and droughts alternating with thunderstorms in Hawai'i.

Other strange things are going on. In the Sierra Nevada Mountains scientists have noted a serious reduction in this year's annual hatch of cabbage butterflies. Cows are producing less milk. Doctors are seeing more dust, mites, and molds, hence more allergies. Gas prices have dropped, surge-protector sales have increased, soft-shelled crabs are less available, and the Earth's rotation has slowed by a tenth of a second. And in Los Angeles (and this is the truth), a man named Al Nino has been getting 2 A.M. phone calls wanting to know why he is screwing up the weather.

Disciplined and observant academics that they are, Kem and Neal don't care a whit about any of this. They believe that something as sacred as an annual golf match should not be trivialized by merely mortal matters like gale-force winds and lethal lightening strikes. So we drive over the Ko'olau Mountains and into the teeth of the perfect storm, and an hour later we arrive at the Kahuku Golf Course, affectionately known to local duffers as "The Goat Pasture," which is located at the very point at which the windward side of the island becomes O'ahu's North Shore. There is absolutely no one else around, so getting a tee time from the manager is easy. We smile and he smiles. His smile, however, also conveys the following meaning: "You stupid *haole* guys don't have a lick of sense and deserve whatever happens to you." We grab raincoats, hats, and umbrellas and commence play.

Kahuku is a nine-hole, par-35 course that is nestled against a wild stretch of ocean. It is a rugged, beautiful place with a proud plantation community surrounding it. The higher fairways, a legacy of those plantation days, adjoin two cemeteries, one near the second hole and the other near the eighth green. Golfers walking near the ocean are often graced with sightings of golden-plovers guarding little pieces of turf or humpback whales rising and sounding across their winter migrations from Alaska.

Today, the nine-hole golf course is made even more stunning by the dark sky, the bent trees, and the windswept thunderheads that are racing across the horizon and discharging torrents of rain as we play. Sudden gusts of wind peel in from the ocean. Large branches fall out of the ironwood trees and seawater splashes up the beach. In this extraordinary setting, Neal and Kem tutor me on the game's finer points and the physics and metaphysics of triumph, failure, and sportsmanship.

"Body and mind must come together in a single effortless movement," says Kem as he hooks one into the ocean with his 7 iron. A second ball follows suit. His third and fourth sail over a small ridge, the last disappearing into a pile of wet sand. "That's right," says Neal, stepping up to his tee. "It's an inner game, Peter, one that will clarify old childhood issues and help get you in touch with your true feelings about women." Neal looks left and right, down and up, swings hard, and bangs one into a tree.

Admittedly, my understanding of these details is simpleminded. As I see it, the fundamental idea is to move your ball around a huge field that has strategically placed obstacles on it, things like massive storm fronts, large rocks, wild pigs, the Pacific Ocean, and other golfers. When you catch up with your ball, you work it into a little hole with one of your skinny clubs and then smack it off again with a fat one so you can't see it anymore. It doesn't matter whether the hole is five feet or five hundred feet away. It all counts the same. So you chase the ball down and do the whole thing over and over again anywhere from 10 to 10,000 times depending on the course you are playing. You try to look cool but work hard not to embarrass yourself too much. That's how Tiger Woods does it, and that's how the three of us are doing it.

Halfway between the third and fourth holes, however, it occurs to me that something as deranged as this game could never have been created in a place like Hawai'i. The ancient *kanaka maoli* were a refined and enlightened people even in their competitive diversions. They (both men and women) boxed, danced hula, bowled *'ulu maika* stones, lassoed sharks from their canoes, shot arrows at rats, threw darts, played wickedly complex board games, and gambled on everything. Nowhere in the historic Polynesian record is there anything quite as self-absorbed and goofy as golf.

Which shouldn't come as a surprise. Though the Dutch have put up some feeble origination claims, golf seems to have developed in Scotland in the fifteenth century. The inventor, someone with entirely too much time on his hands, had incredible insight into the human psyche. He (feminists have conceded that it must have been a man) figured out that people could frustrate themselves forever with nothing more than a round pebble, a rabbit burrow, and a mallet of driftwood. Mind you, the Scots like these sorts of challenges. These are the same people who to this day annually toss large boulders and tall telephone poles around in their Highland competitions.

Odd as it may be cross-culturally, it is the game of golf rather than the more ancient sports of *'ulu maika* or spear throwing that has captured the hearts and minds of Hawai'i's visitors. People come from all over the world to play on our seventy-five different courses, especially in winter. Usually, it is the big private fairways that draw the traffic, places like Kapalua on Maui, Wai'alae on O'ahu, or Princeville on Kaua'i. A few visitors end up at the Volcano Golf and Country Club on the Big Island where play is routinely interrupted by gaggles of wild Hawaiian geese or the odd covey of pheasants waddling across the greens. Others gravitate to Ko'olau Golf Course, the most challenging and scenic in Hawai'i, and maybe in the world.

Like their international counterparts, local golfers play with dedication and passion. Hawai'i, in fact, is one of the most golf-o-centric places in the world. As often as not, ordinary local people go to the cheaper public courses like Kahuku Municipal where we are now playing. Under normal conditions, Kahuku's gently rolling landscape would be bathed in sunlight and soothed by balmy trade winds. The fairways, naturally bumpy because of the rough grass that has been planted to tolerate salt air, would be teeming with small-business proprietors, college students, housewives, and retired schoolteachers.

But today is a different matter altogether. The ground is soggy. The wind is howling. The air is laden with sand particles. Holes four, seven, and eight, which all run along the shoreline and usually offer commanding views, are occluded by a wind-chopped sea. Water, mist, and foam are being hurled into the air and far above the high-water line. Across the entire course, there is a great emptiness. We are entirely, totally, incomparably alone, which just maybe should be a source of concern.

The gentlemen I am golfing with, however, take all this in stride. No ordinary golfers, these. They have transcended and are oblivious to the elements including the massive lagoon that is slowly forming under our feet. "Golf," says Kem professorially as he addresses the ball with a smile, "is a part of the human capacity that is waiting in all of us to be born. It is ontologically, epistemologically, cosmologically, and phenomenologically significant." With a flourish, he brings his number 3 wood back and cuts a perfect arc to the tee. There is a satisfying "thwack" and the ball surges off on a straight trajectory to the next hole.

As he finishes his swing, however, the club slips through his fingers, turns end over end in a somersault, and sails between Neal's head and mine, missing both of us by inches. "Nice shot," says Neal. Meanwhile, I tee up, push my hat back, take a colossal swing, and watch my ball dribble off the peg and roll into a puddle. I try again. The ball goes another three feet. "Just throw 'em already," says one of my teachers. I whack it one more time and this time slice it into the surf. "It all comes down to life, liberty, and the pursuit of golf balls," says Neal, who teaches political science. He has studied these matters for many years and is a great role model.

For the next hour, then, we traverse the remaining holes of the Kahuku course and work our way back up toward the parking lot where we started. As we approach the ninth hole, however, a miracle occurs. The rain stops, the cloud cover parts and sunlight actually starts to stream down onto the course. I do some quick mental calculations and estimate that each of us is somewhere in the range of 270 over par. Larry, Moe, and Curly playing miniature golf in the Mir space station couldn't have done better.

"Our game was a tad off today," says Neal. "Yep," says Kem, "it's because we didn't bring the right clubs." Personally, I tell them, its because of "the boy child." El Niño, so I have read, caused the Black Death of 1340 and the French Revolution of 1789. Surely it has thrown off today's game. It's the perfect excuse. When El Niño disappears we can blame it on computer crashes and delayed effects from the Year 2000 bug.

The course manager, who has been listening and watching this, has a different view. "You guys might want to stay in town and try some bowling next time." We thank him for the tip, stow our clubs and rain gear in the trunk, and head back to town, at peace with ourselves in golf paradise.

Sushi Man

A small confession. I have a strange affection for odd and improbable machines. Trains, planes, and cars from the early 1900s instantly attract my eye. Old tanks, jeeps, and boats and, on a smaller scale, old typewriters, gum ball machines, and automatic coin counters qualify because their form and function seem—well, goofy. So too do certain bicycles, camp stoves, meat grinders, and aluminum can squashers. In kinder moments, my wife and daughters call this a "guy thing." At other times they attribute it to that certain moment years ago when we were hiking and I smacked my head on a low-hanging branch.

Actually, this infatuation for peculiar contraptions started at age 8 when I read Robert McCloskey's story about Homer Price. Homer was a kid my age who lived in an imaginary town called Centerburg, USA. In one adventure, Homer's Uncle Ulysses buys a new doughnut-making machine for his lunchroom. He sees it as a "labor saving device." Ulysses assembles it wrong, the machine goes berserk, and millions of doughnuts spew out. I loved it!

With a curiosity verging on the freaky, then, I recently got wind of a new sushi-making machine at an all-you-can-eat Japanese restaurant here in Honolulu called Jan Jan. Sushi may be trendy stuff in other climes, but in Hawai'i it is a dietary staple. Sushi is the staff and stuff of life. We eat the little morsels for lunch, dinner, and as a snack, and we tend to get quite fussy if not downright belligerent about what constitutes a proper piece of sushi.

So the idea of a sushi-making machine immediately struck me as peculiar and rife with possibilities. Forthwith, I called up Mr. Bailey Kuewa, Jan Jan's assistant manager, and put it to him directly: "May I come down right now and see your sushi machine?" "Absolutely," he responded. "It's cranking 'em out as we speak."

Then, on the way over to Jan Jan, it suddenly hit me. A sushi machine? Machines don't make sushi. Machines mash stuff. They transport, aggregate, convey, and purvey solid materials. They crunch, grind, roll, push, and pulverize things. They build, pick, roll, move, remove, cut, add, count, slice, or otherwise control inanimate objects. But not sushi. Sushi is a delicacy, an elegant little Japanese morsel that is made with steamed rice infused with vinegar and sugar and served with bite-sized pieces of fish or vegetable. Sushi is a craft, a bricolage, and, in its ultimate perfection, an art. And machines? Well—they are just machines.

Or are they? Bailey escorted me directly into the kitchen to inspect the sushi maker. It was a nondescript affair, about the size of a water cooler and made of plastic and enamel. It bore an assortment of electronic buttons and dials. One of the cooks, Tomoo Saotome, was scooping hot rice into the top of the machine. Little oblong sushis were dropping out the bottom. Saotome twiddled a knob and soon each sushi was also getting a little squirt of wasabi, the green horseradish that adds flavor and snap.

As Saotome dressed his freshly minted sushi with pieces of shrimp and scallop, I asked him about the machine's background. "Ah," he said with obvious reverence, "sushi robot is made by Tomoe Company in Japan." The counter on the robot read 9,268. Another four dropped out of the robot and the meter jumped to 9,272. Saotome offered me one. Not bad.

Still, the sushi "robot" wasn't exactly what I thought it would be. It seemed too futuristic, too avant garde, as if the next model might require all of us to settle for sushi space pellets designed by NASA for weightless environments. Recognizing my obvious interest in rice ball making, though, Bailey suggested that I drop in at another place that was undergoing rapid mechanization. Genki Sushi over on Kapahulu Avenue not only used a sushi robot, it delivered the finished product to customers on a conveyor belt. I drove over, entered Genki's, and made for an empty seat.

Sure enough. Genki's is a place for industrial-style sushi eating. I squeezed into a group of thirty other customers who were pulling plates off the moving sushi sidewalk. The place was absolutely silent. Everyone was hunkered over their piece of the counter nibbling at sushi fresh off the belt. Waitresses scuttled back and forth with refills of green tea. Lips smacked. A woman next to me slurped her tea. Chopsticks clicked. Someone burped.

Meanwhile, a vast parade of sushi passed in front of me. All Japanese cooking emphasizes variety and presentation and sushi is no different. The seaweed wraps must be the proper kind, dry and crisp. Fish and vegetables are to be fresh. Pickled, sliced ginger must accompany sushi as a condiment. The rice must be cooked and vinegared just so and the tea that is served must be green and bitter.

Great consideration also goes into the food that adorns sushi. Horse mackerel, mushrooms, spinach, water chestnuts, conger eel, radish sprouts, gizzard shad, herring roe, abalone, marbled tuna belly, razor-shell clam, young sea bass, and squid simmered in soy stock are all rolled, pressed, or draped on the rice. You may, however, find these ingredients in unusual combinations: sweet egg custard wrapped in dried seaweed, slices of cucumber inside rice coated with sesame seeds, and rice dolloped with sea urchin roe.

But even as a long convoy of empty sushi plates disappeared into a kitchen window on Genki's conveyor system, I realized something was amiss. Don't misunderstand me. In the brave new world of global cookery, sushi machines and moving food sidewalks are entertaining and functional. But where, I wondered, is the artistry? Where is the much-vaunted magic that is supposed to occur when a real sushi maker confronts raw ingredients and plies his craft? And could a highly trained sushi chef do better than a twenty-first-century gizmo?

A few days later, I learned the answer. My friend Junko Maeda, Kem Lowry's wife, was born in Fukuoka. She grew up in Tokyo but has now lived most of her life in Hawai'i. Junko knows sushi the way guys like me know burgers and fries. And, in my quest for a bona fide sushi man, she knew exactly where to take me: a place called Sushi Masa run by proprietor, chef, and sushi master Masa Nakayama.

Junko introduced us and Masa bowed slightly and invited us to sit down. Masa is a tall and handsome man in his early 50s. Dressed in immaculate white cooking clothes, he stood directly behind the sushi bar and showed us some of the day's fish, which included several local tunas, imported mackerel, salmon, and some fine-looking shellfish. As we talked, I learned that he grew up in Tokyo in a family of professional seafood brokers. His father had tried to discourage him from becoming a sushi chef because he thought the work was too demanding. Nonetheless, Masa eventually studied under his older brother, who worked in various other Tokyo restaurants and became a master of the trade.

With that as background, Masa moved into his work. He began with a simple "maguro." Taking a choice piece of raw tuna, Masa carefully sliced four identical and perfectly shaped pieces. Then he reached into a large pot, peeled off a ball of rice, and deftly rolled it into the traditional oblong shape. Next he dipped a finger in a bowl of wasabi, spread it on the tuna, pressed the tuna into the rice, and arranged two pieces on the wooden platter in front of me. "Always two pieces to a serving," he told us, "the first to taste, the second to savor."

The moment of truth had come. Images flashed in front of me. The Tomoe Sushi Robot as steam hammer—Masa as John Henry. Rocky Balboa versus all of the equipment in the gym. Sushi Man versus Sushi Machine.

Masa showed me how to eat a sushi the proper way. Use your fingers, grasp it firmly, turn it upside down, dip the fish part in soy sauce and wasabi, and shove the whole thing in your mouth. No nibbling or dabbling and no chopsticks. Then Junko and I gave them the taste test: truly exquisite, a blend of rich tastes, contrasting textures, and subtle flavors.

For the next two hours I ate and pondered sushi while Junko interpreted the nuances. Effortlessly, Master Nakayama produced perfection after perfection. Most were traditional sushi made with *unagi* (eel), *amaebi* (shrimp), and *ikura* (salmon egg), but to each he would add some small flourish: a special cut of the fish, a folded vegetable, a unique arrangement on the plate. All were prepared in front of us, a tradition and formality that guarantees customers they are eating the very freshest food made by someone who knows what he is doing. In the old days, unscrupulous sushi chefs would use older fish or wilted but reconstituted vegetables. Cooking everything immediately in front of the customer, he explained, allows the customer to appreciate the art of the making.

Excellence in the sushi trade, Masa says, requires a chef to work with the available fish and shellfish of the season. It is a point of honor. A true sushi chef will attentively select components that please both eye and palate. Then, he said, the ingredients must be treated with great care. It is a matter of preserving the freshness and taste of food that spoils easily. Even so, sushi is a time- and labor-intensive craft. It demands discipline and attention to detail because each sushi has its own form. Most young people, Masa told us, have no patience for it. An apprentice is required to sweep floors, wash dishes, and make deliveries. Eventually, he will be allowed to cook rice or boil eggs. "You must steal the knowledge from your teacher," explains Masa. By this, he means that the burden is on the student to learn rather than on the teacher to teach.

At Masa's sushi bar, there are no robots and conveyor belts and I suspect there never will be. Masa's art is based on sharp knives, clean pots, a deep reservoir of food knowledge, and an instinct for the artistic. I asked Masa if sushi chefs meet and talk with each other. "Do you go to sushi chef conferences?" Junko chuckled at my question but he said, "Yes, we have an organization, but we never divulge our special secrets and recipes to each other."

As dinner drew to a close, one of those special sushi creations materialized before us. Masa took a slice of smoked salmon (the precise recipe for smoking is his secret), a piece of prime tuna, and a sliver of avocado. He placed them in a rice ball. Then, he wrapped the sushi in dried seaweed and carefully dipped it in tempura batter and then into hot oil. It came to us lightly fried, crisp on the outside, luxurious and ever so smooth and delicate on the inside.

At the end of the evening Masa offered us homemade green tea ice cream, rich and thick and dabbed with plum wine and wasabi. An odd combination, I thought, and one that seemed counterintuitive: the sweetness of the wine, the creaminess of the ice cream, the sharp snap of the wasabi. With great subtlety and delicacy, it worked.

Two hours later, we were still lingering over hot tea. I explained the legend of John Henry to Masa and Junko and thanked them both for sharing their knowledge. "There is no machine in the world that can do all this," said Junko with an enigmatic smile. "Not yet," I heard Masa say. He smiled, I bowed, and then we departed in silence.

10

The Neighbors Drop In

The house we live in, the house that roots us to the island we live on, is located on the floor of Mānoa Valley. Mānoa is a splendid place to live. The valley's fluted walls shelter us and gauzy, cliff-hanging mists quench our thirst for beauty. Old homes speak to us of history. Knowledge and friendship with neighbors make for community. Mānoa is stately and imperturbable, a fine place to live, to visit, or simply to hang out for a time. But those of us who dwell here also know that things occasionally go haywire.

Saturday evening. It is quiet and we are basking in the afterglow of a fine day. A dog is yipping somewhere in the distance. Its bark carries loosely on trade winds that are rustling through the big avocado tree in the backyard. A few cars pass by and there are muffled voices from some neighbors a few doors down. Other than that, it is still.

A few minutes after 10 P.M., Kelly, our youngest daughter, is in her room. She is talking on the phone with her cousin Alyssa. They are discussing sunburns, boyfriends, and the humpback whale count they have just completed for a school project. Carolyn is in the living room curled up in a chair. She is reading a book and sipping tea. I am in the bedroom and on the very edge of conking off.

Suddenly, the tranquility explodes. From the front of the house on Mānoa Road, there is a stupendous roar and, just behind it, the kaleidoscopic reverberations of a crash. It happens in a split second, but we experience it in a harsh series of slow-motion frames. First it is quiet. Then the silence fractures. In the next instant wood splinters, glass shatters, metal grates and crunches against stone, plastic implodes, and the house shudders and settles.

I leap out of bed not quite sure what is going on but knowing that whatever it is, it has to be bad. Kelly screams. Carolyn yells something that I can't understand. In the seconds that follow, all the various sounds and movements blur together. Carolyn goes for the front door. I run into the kitchen. We pass each other and then see the same thing from different angles.

A car has come down the hill above us and punched through into our kitchen. Where a wall and window existed just moments before, I can now see the grill, headlights, and smashed windshield of a 1990 Jaguar. The kitchen is full of debris. Our refrigerator has tipped over and food is spilling out. Lights are flickering. I hear the sound of water gushing from a burst pipe and smell what I think may be gas.

I tear around the corner to find Carolyn. She is just outside the front door helping two people out of the Jaguar that is sticking out of our house. "Call 911," she yells. I get the police on the line, give them our address, and then help Carolyn bring the two occupants of the car inside. It is Sam and Mary Cooke, people who live up the valley a little way and folks we know. They are shaken but unhurt.

So too with Carolyn, Kelly, and me. In short order, police, firemen, and paramedics show up. A crowd of neighbors, some curious, some concerned, quickly gathers. Mānoa Road is blocked off with squad cars. I find the right valves and fuses and shut off the water and electricity. People gawk and point and Sam and I talk to the firemen and police. Soon, a tow truck arrives to start the hour-long task of extracting the Jag from the wall of our house. Everyone stands well away as the car is wrenched out and hauled off.

Sam, of course, is deeply mortified. He and Mary apologize over and over. As the story unfolds, it is even more amazing that nobody is injured or dead. Sam and Mary had gone to visit their good friends the Burgesses, who live just up the hill from us. After a pleasant dinner, they got in their car, which was facing downhill. Sam backed it up a few feet and then put it in gear. The car suddenly accelerated. He thinks it may have hit 55 or 60 mph when it crossed Mānoa Road and slammed into our house.

Over the next few hours, the adrenaline and excitement fade. Three of the firemen help me push the broken refrigerator upright. Then they and the police make their reports and leave. Neighbors and passing onlookers drift away and Sam and Mary walk home. Then Carolyn, Kelly, and I are alone. We clean up the worst of the food and broken glass that is piled knee deep in the kitchen. In the wee hours of the morning, we turn in, exhausted.

A few hours later, at first light, I go out to survey the carnage. The path of destruction is worse than I realized. Our house looks vaguely like Jurassic Park after the dinosaurs got loose. Before it embedded itself in the house, the Jag-o-saurus tore through a rock wall, sheared off a six-foot mock orange hedge, ripped our lime tree out by its roots, knocked down some of our laundry area, and destroyed most of a hundred-year-old stone gatepost with the property's name engraved in Hawaiian. The entire house is now deflected, leaning off plumb about five degrees.

I start piling up splintered boards and broken roof and laundry room parts. Under some shards of masonry, I find the twisted remains of a bread maker that was sitting on a shelf in the kitchen. Pieces of kitchen wall lie in a mangled mess and chunks of quarried blue stone from the wall are strewn across the front, broken into little pieces as if they were crackers. Some of the beautiful, sixty-year-old, straight-grained two-by-four interior studs are protruding from the house. This kind of wood isn't milled anymore and even the blue stone is hard to find.

Looking around, I feel depressed at the devastation and wonder how in the world all this can be made right. Inside, Carolyn is also up. She is rummaging through the remains of the kitchen. I go inside to help her. The rug in the living room is full of small bits of glass and tracked with muddy skid marks. And where the Jag-o-saurus was hanging like a wall trophy at the Hard Rock Cafe, there is now a gaping six foot by six foot hole looking out onto the street. Carolyn is stoic, but I know she is also crestfallen at the sight our home of twenty-five years in pieces.

Pretty soon, though, a car rolls up. A little voice says, "Hi, Uncle." It's our good friends, Tom and Wilma Ogimi and their daughter Tricia, who is a kind of "calabash" niece because all of our kids went to the same school and grew up together. Wilma and Carolyn jog together four times a week. They've brought coffee and pastries for breakfast. Then another car comes along. It's Sam and Mary and their friends the Burgesses, come to inspect the damage and lend a hand. Dennis Sugihara, my wife's classmate from high school, comes by. A short while later, Claire Matsumoto, who is Wilma's sister and who lives across the street and a few doors down, also drops by. She has a small refrigerator in tow on a hand truck. "You'll need this," she says with a smile, "and you can return it whenever."

By midmorning, things start to look better.

Other neighbors like George Freitas and his wife Dot wander by to offer commiseration or a bit of help. So too does Daisy Kurashige, who is the neighborhood's best gardener and who immediately inspects the flattened hedge and lime tree looking for signs of life. She shakes her head in disbelief. Bruce Mau walks by with his two little boys, who are trying to behave themselves but who actually think all this havoc is kind of neat.

Then Carolyn's folks, Tetsui and Alice Watanabe, arrive bearing mops and dustpans. I call Diamond Head Plumbing to come out and restore water and they send a man named Clayton, who turns out to be a friend of an old friend who retired from the plumbing business years ago. Meanwhile, my brother-in-law Tom Tyler and his wife Kathy, who is Carolyn's sister, swing by in their pickup. Tom tapes up the dangling electrical outlets and then we switch the full power back on.

Next, we brace the roof and plug the Jag-o-saurus hole with a large piece of plywood. Carolyn's brother Roger brings a bunch of coolers over to store food. Her other brother, Brent, puts plastic sheets over the plywood patch and seals everything up with his staple gun. Then, late in the day, Ted Tsukiyama, another relative (and a fellow Mānoa Valley resident), is driving by. He sees me shoveling debris into bags, stops, rolls down his window, and says: "Hey, Adler, must have been a hell of a party. How come you never invite me?"

Over the next few days, word of the accident spreads around town. Honolulu is a small place with its own peculiar circuit board of gossip. Little towns in Illinois or Iowa are the same way, as are certain neighborhoods in big cities like Los Angeles or New York. People in intact communities always gather when someone's car is stuck in the snow, when the barn must be raised, the hay brought in, or the community center repaired. Eventually, of course, it had to happen. My friend and colleague Audrey calls me and asks if I've heard the news: "Our beloved Sam and Mary Cooke almost died when their car smashed into someone's house in Mānoa."

That same day, sorting through the last of the rubble, I uncover a polished cement plate that used to be fixed in the middle of the old rock gate post. It is chipped but still intact and has our address on it. It is a beautiful piece of stone with a warm, incandescent look that harkens back to the last century when our front step was the entrance to an old estate. I set it upright on the front steps and Kelly puts some flowers around it. In the weeks ahead, we will rebuild the post and put it back in place. For the moment, though, it is enough to have it standing prominent on the steps where we sometimes like to meet or greet the people who live near us. The name engraved on the stone says "Luana Pua." It means "enjoyment of the flowers."

11

Harbor Moves

Each morning before the sun comes up, Alan Sandrey leaves his home in Waipahu and makes his way across the central plain of O'ahu to go to work. When he reaches his destination, he parks his car, takes an elevator to the tenth floor, enters a small room, makes some coffee, settles into a high-backed chair, and picks up a pair of high-powered binoculars. Slowly, he scans the shimmering waters of Honolulu Harbor looking for trouble.

Sandrey has a peculiar but interesting job. He is a marine traffic controller and his specific role is to shunt some twenty ships a day around Sand Island, through the main ship channel, and in and out of Honolulu Harbor. The "office" from which he does all this maneuvering is a small, instrumented room with outdoor balconies overlooking much of the city's waterfront. It sits high atop Aloha Tower, which is the historic centerpiece of Honolulu's recently revitalized waterfront.

Most days, if there is no impending crisis, Sandrey will brew his pot of coffee, check the orange cone and ball day signals on the tower's yardarms, settle into a swivel chair, and twiddle the knobs on two VHF radios. He will start talking to different ships' captains or pilots, some of whom are at sea waiting to come in, others of whom are in port queuing up to get out. All of them depend entirely on his approval to move around the harbor. If things go right, it's smooth sailing. If something goes wrong, a ship could conceivably end up on Bishop Street in the middle of downtown traffic.

Aloha Tower, with its unparalleled view of the waterfront, is an appropriately nautical spot from which to do this kind of maritime choreography. The entire area is filled with ocean-related activities that draw millions of visitors a year. In addition to fine stores and restaurants, there are rides on the historic fireboat *Abner T. Longley* and turns aboard the four-masted merchant ship *Falls of Clyde*. There are visits to the Hawai'i Maritime Center, which is dedicated exclusively to Hawai'i's multifaceted seafaring legacy, and tours of the double-hulled sailing canoe *Hōkūle'a* built by the Polynesian Voyaging Society to revive open-ocean voyages to Tahiti, New Zealand, and Rapa Nui.

Aloha Tower stands tall in the middle of all this. Constructed in 1924, the 184-feet, 2-inch high structure houses a seven-ton clock with faces aimed at all four points of the compass. In the 1930s, luxury liners like the *Lurline* and the SS *Monterey* would tie up beside the tower with great fanfare after the two-week trip from San Francisco or Los Angeles. Kids dove for coins and flower leis bedecked the newly arrived. Today, modern cruise ships are returning to both the Aloha Tower and to the surrounding Aloha Tower Marketplace.

But Honolulu Harbor, with its fifty-three piers, thirty berthing facilities, and 130 acres of container yards, is, first and foremost, a working port. In fact, Port of Honolulu, Sandrey tells me, is known to maritime people worldwide as the "7-11 of the Pacific," a place to bunker fuel, transship cargo, resupply foodstores, find a doctor, repair a ballast tank, or just take in a movie if you've been at sea for a month.

On the day I visit him, Sandrey checks two large clipboards over his desk to see what is on the schedule. The blue clipboard logs international ship movements, the yellow one interisland traffic. Even as he does this, things are stirring out on the water. Two ships want to leave at the same time. The *Chief Gadao* is ready to depart with a load of cargo. So is the tug *Lopaka,* which is pulling a small submersible called *Voyager I* out of Pier 41. Sandrey talks with both vessels, brokers different departure times, and turns his attention to a fully laden grain ship and two long-liners waiting for ingress.

Sandrey, the harbor's official "traffic-meister," isn't the only one charged with keeping things orderly and moving. David Lyman, a fifth-generation *kanaka maoli*-Chinese-Caucasian seaman with a bushy mustache and an encyclopedic knowledge of local maritime lore, is one of nine licensed harbor pilots. He and his colleagues are responsible for the tactical navigations that get large ships through narrow channels and into skinny berths. The job is something akin to parallel parking an eighteen-foot car in an eighteen-and-a-half-foot parking space on a busy, two-way side street.

On the day I visit him, Lyman is scheduled to bring the Matson containership *Manukai* into Pier 53 from an offshore holding point just outside the harbor. The 721-foot *Manukai,* three and one-half days out from San Francisco, is skippered by Captain Alan Thoma. It has a gross of 23,786 tons and a draft of 34 feet. She is carrying a crew of twenty-eight and nearly a thousand containers of general freight. There are refrigerated vegetables picked and packed five days ago in Salinas Valley, tanks full of corn syrup, crates of tools and machine parts, loads of paper towels and vacuum cleaners, stacked rows of PVC piping, a freezer container full of ice cream, and three containers carrying live, squealing pigs.

Lyman, wearing baggy shorts, an old aloha shirt, tennis shoes, and a British Columbia pilot's cap (exchanged for a Honolulu counterpart at a recent harbor pilot convention), is driven out to the *Manukai* in the bright yellow powerboat that the pilots use as a water taxi. On the way out, we thread our way through miscellaneous water traffic and pass several outrigger canoes from the WaikīkīSurf Club, Sean Martin and Jim Cook's *Pacific Dream*, the long-liner *E.T.* headed into port with a load of swordfish, and a half dozen pleasure craft out fishing, sunning, and sailing.

In response to some of my queries about matters nautical, Lyman cautions me about interchanging the words "ship" and "boat." Sea captains tend to be touchy about these things, he explains. When we are on board the *Manukai,* he directs me to use the word "ship." The rule of thumb for landlubbers is that you can carry a boat inside a ship but you can't haul a ship inside a boat. I have a lot of technical questions about this little rule of thumb, but Lyman laughs and says not to worry about it. "Captain Thoma is a forgiving sort."

As we come alongside the containership, a fifteen-foot rope ladder is lowered and, hand over hand, we climb up the swaying port side of the *Manukai.* We are welcomed by Chief Mate Michael Mociun and taken up three decks to the bridge. Captain Dave and Captain Al greet each other and exchange a few stories. Al talks about the voyage over, Dave about a recent trip to England. Then, Dave lights a cigar, sips from a cup of coffee that has materialized in his hand courtesy of a crew member, and goes over the docking plan.

There are jokes, stories, and the easy banter of seamen who know their trade. Then, it's on to the business at hand. Dave radios Sandrey up in the tower, gets permission to proceed, and directs the *Manukai* to advance at slow speed. "We're inbound," he reports on the radio. Slowly, the ship works its way forward. Soon, two tugs, the *Mī'oi* and the *'Eleu*, link up, one on the forward starboard side, the other at the stern. The tugs come alongside and tie up to the *Manukai* with huge hawsers even as she starts working her way at slow speed into Honolulu Harbor.

Three sets of engines, two from the tugs and one from the containership, now control the ship's motion. Lyman, affable and at ease but acutely attentive to every twitch of the ship, keeps up a constant conversation with the tugboat captains by radio. Now and then, he gives directions to Captain Thoma and Chief Mate Mociun to ease back the speed or bear farther port or starboard. The *Manukai* creeps forward.

In theory, a ship's captain has ultimate responsibility for his craft. He could countermand an order from a pilot but it almost never happens. Aside from the fact that all harbor pilots are intimately familiar with their own waters, Dave and Al are both from the Islands and have worked together for twenty years. So it is now Dave who must place the ship against Pier 53 where cranes and gantries are waiting to off-load the *Manukai*'s containers and reload it with eastbound containers.

Creeping through the harbor, we pass dozens of ships in the strange, mixed-up fleet that calls Honolulu Harbor home. We see low-riding fuel barges and squat oceangoing tugs. We pass the crisp, white Coast Guard cutters *Jarvis* and *Rush* and the black buoy tenders *Mallow* and *Sassafras*. We see the sugar ship *Moku Pahu,* the oceanographic research vessel *Townsend Cromwell,* and the fireboat *Moku ʻAhi.* We go by a large dinner-cruise catamaran, the *Aliʻi Kai,* and then let loose with a long, ear-ringing blast of the foghorn (which I have the honor of triggering) as we pass the liner *Independence,* fresh in from Kauaʻi and tied up at Pier 10 next to the Aloha Tower. Someone at the Marketplace responds by ringing a bell.

Then, ever so slowly, Dave brings the *Manukai* up to Pier 53 and begins to direct the tugs as they angle the containership forward and sideways into the dock. It is all about Newtonian physics and the careful business of moving a dense mass of slow-moving ship through a limited quantum of time and space. More unvoiced maneuvering images come to me. Balancing on a high wire above Niagara Falls while holding two bags of groceries. Walking on the ledge of a building while holding onto a small child. Squeezing an overweight cat through a mouse hole.

The last fifteen feet involved in bringing the *Manukai* dockside take twenty minutes. Dave delicately directs speed, angle, and momentum. It is an elaborate, complex process requiring precision timing and split-second decision making. In the end, it is all about the mastery of craft and the merging of art and science.

Suddenly, we are in. Lines are secured. There's a bit of paperwork to be completed and then the gangway is lowered and all of us troop off the ship as the stevedores board to commence discharge. Cranes swing into place. Holds are opened. Crates are unstrapped and the men and women who work the docks swarm across the ship in a determined, syncopated rhythm that is practiced daily.

Up in Aloha Tower, Sandrey has tracked the movement of the *Manukai* through the channel, into the harbor, and alongside her berth. It is now late morning. Visitors from Osaka, Kansas City, Calgary, and Mexico City are thronging through the Marketplace. Quite a few of them will take the elevator up to the top of the tower and see Sandrey talking on his radio or pacing one of the balconies. Some will also have watched the *Manukai* come in. As for Captains Lyman and Thoma, they will soon be adjourning to the Aloha Marketplace for lunch, stories, and a continuing stream of salt-encrusted observations about narrow escapes and the life and times around Honolulu Harbor. There will be a few fibs and exaggerations mixed in, but most of what they talk about is the truth.

12

The Sound of Frozen Fire

Hawai'i is incomparably visual. Look *makai* from the land to the ocean and you see an indigo sea and blue-green surf rolling up long stretches of beach. Turn *mauka* (the other way, toward the mountains) and you confront green valleys carpeted with rain forest and nestled beneath the sawtooth profile of volcanic mountains. Look up and you are encompassed by a crystalline sky. Look around (with a smile) and you will see the beautiful faces of Polynesia, Asia, and America smiling back unless you happen to have come to Hawai'i with less than good motive. On any given day, the eye absorbs a thousand bits of beauty and still never sees them all.

But Hawai'i has sounds to match. Some—the lilt of pidgin the first time you hear it—catch your ear and playfully tug at your mind. Others, a rainstorm borne on fast-moving trades or the gong of a bell from a neighborhood Buddhist temple, reverberate long after the moment has passed. But every once in a while some peculiar combination of tones, pitches, and notes captures what is essential about Hawai'i and conveys it in a startling, new manner.

It's Sunday afternoon. A lanky 31-year-old man with tousled hair named Donald R. Womack is sitting in the first row of the balcony of the Neil S. Blaisdell Concert Hall in Honolulu. Womack is one of 2,000 people listening expectantly—and, in his case, apprehensively—as one of those new sounds materializes. At that very moment, in fact, the Honolulu Symphony under the able direction of Samuel Wong is playing the first bars of a short, specially commissioned orchestral piece called "On Fields of Frozen Fire."

The composition is all about Hawai'i and everyone is intensely curious what it will be like. Conductor Wong raises his baton and pauses. The musicians stand ready, lips pursed over mouthpieces, bows holding steady on the strings. After a long pause, Wong's baton descends and the first notes are played. The notes are clearly not what people expect and the disappointment is instant, audible, palpable, and visible. I have to admit that I would rather be at the beach or up in the mountains or just about anyplace else myself.

Generally speaking, symphonic openings tend to be rich, melodic, and suggestive of some discernable theme. Openings set a tone, create a mood, or lay tracks for where a composer plans to take things. Think, for example, of the beginning of the great orchestral works by Beethoven, Mozart, or Liszt. Or, if you prefer, ponder the opening bars from music by John Philip Sousa, Elvis Presley, or your own local barbershop quartet. Introductions create an aperture or portal. They begin things and define what will come. They are supposed to open the mind, the senses, and your feelings.

The chords of "On Fields of Frozen Fire" are just the opposite. They are austere, desolate, and atonal. They start nowhere, go nowhere, are confused in between, and seem to shut things down. Like good listeners, however, we wait for the next few lines. They come in the form of a powerful beat from the timpani interrupting the strings. The audience is jolted further.

For something that is supposed to be about gracious, easy-going Hawai'i, this is a peculiar and notably sour beginning. It is forbidding, disquieting, and alien and no one knows what to make of it. People fidget. Programs rustle. There are muffled coughs and not so subtle throat clearings. Arms fold. Legs cross. People shake their heads, quietly cluck to their companions, or inspect their nails.

Donald Womack has better reasons than most to be agitated. He is the man who has composed "On Fields of Frozen Fire" and, along with the hall full of people, is hearing its world premiere. To make matters worse, his piece is a prelude to two musical heavyweights. The first is the rapturous and exceedingly difficult Concerto no. 3 by Rachmaninoff, which is the piece at the center of the movie *Shine.* That will be followed by Richard Strauss' *Also Sprach Zarathustra,* the opening notes of which are best remembered from Stanley Kubrik's science fiction film *2001.*

In the balcony, Womack is in obvious distress. Much of his agony comes from that roving and predacious swarm of butterflies that attacks the gastric systems of young artists unveiling important works. Most painters, writers, and musicians survive the jitters of a major debut and look back on them later as a formative experience. Those that don't, hope for posthumous recognition or declare it a moral victory and move on to another line of work.

But the burden of a young, classical musician in the 50th State is a bit heavier, even on opening night. If you are doing "long hair," Honolulu is a tough town to play. Mind you, we residents of the 50th State bear no special hostility toward cellos, piccolos, and harpsichords. In fact, Hawai'i has a venerable tradition of classical music and a surprisingly large group of symphony devotees. There is also a small caucus of symphonic extremists who insist that we should be ranked ahead of London, New York, and Vienna.

Such arguments are rarely voiced in front of someone like Womack. Islands tend to be polite places. No one intentionally wants to hurt the feelings of anyone else and, like any other small community, people will forgive (even if they don't forget). Still, most people in Hawai'i understand that the average visitor from Asia or America does not travel to Hawai'i to listen to Tchaikovsky. To the contrary, most of the local music scene centers on a thriving Hawaiian music industry. Hawaiian music is lyrical, melodic, and poetic. Jazz, country, salsa, heavy metal, and New Age all have their place, but local ears are more attendant to the strums of slack key guitars and the soft plinkings of ukuleles. Bassoons, violas, and triangles are the exception.

So Womack has a tough job. But as his piece evolves, the audience begins to join with the music. It isn't a perfect match, but arms unfold and people lean forward to catch the nuances. Patterns and rhythms emerge. An English horn and bass clarinet do solos. Then, ever so slowly, the inspiration and meaning of "On Fields of Frozen Fire" begins to take form. The transformation is visible and Womack's story is now one that people in the concert hall recognize.

To understand this palpable and growing comprehension, turn the clock back a year. Donald and his wife Anna are driving across the Kohala district on the island of Hawai'i. Womack, a native of Tennessee, came to Hawai'i in 1994 to take a job as a junior professor of music composition at the University of Hawai'i. His wife Anna is also a skilled musician. She has found work as a cellist with the Honolulu Symphony.

On their first trip around the Big Island, they discover what so many others before them have. They are stunned by Kohala's thick jungles and forests, the old and decrepit (but still alive) plantation towns, the high waterfalls and sweeping seascapes, and the gnarled and crumpled lava lands. Then, driving by one particular flow, Donald gets out of his car to take a closer look. He picks his way across and, in the folds of one trough, finds new plants taking root. They are lichens, ferns, and the seedlings of certain endemic shrubs that are always the first life to inhabit a fresh lava flow.

Donald and Anna are absorbed by the textures and colors, but, even more, Donald is mesmerized by the odd combination of desolation and fertility. Understand, of course, that to venture across these trenches of Hawaiian lava with an inquiring mind is to journey back in time. Not just the everyday time we count in minutes or months, but the kind of "deep time" that is measured in epochs. Standing there, Womack is touched by something centuries old.

So, like the very spores and seeds that are colonizing this new land, an idea takes root. In Honolulu a month later, Donald leaves his cozy, music-filled apartment on the edge of Waikīkī and goes for an early morning run. Jogging along the beach and still brooding on his expedition across the lava, a first musical line comes to him. He works it around in his mind and commits it to memory. A mile later as he rounds Diamond Head, he composes a second line. By the end of the run, the core ideas of "Frozen Fire" have germinated.

Womack is a disciplined and determined composer. He begins to craft his work, building on previous compositions and toying with different notions that can express his thoughts and feelings about the fierce power rising up from the land. Foremost in his mind is the strange alchemy of turbulence and beauty that attends the birth of an island. But how to express it acoustically?

After creating his spartan, symbolic opening with the strings and timpani, Donald develops two musical motifs. The first is a traditional Hawaiian chant called "Aia O Pele I Hawai'i" described to him by an ethnomusicologist at the university. The chant celebrates the tempestuous volcano goddess Pele. The second is more illusive. It is a long and subtle duet of sounds in which little ordinary ideas of beauty are suddenly overcome or submerged by powerful forces only to rise again in new form.

Over the next six months, with plenty of encouragement and consultation from Anna, the two motifs become major themes. They merge in the music and, six days before finishing his composition, he is also inspired to write a poem that can accompany the composition. As Womack describes it, "On Fields of Frozen Fire" is all about conflict and resolution. "It reflects on the nature of the lava fields and the contrasts which they embody—fire out of water, beauty in the midst of desolation, destruction which leads to the rebirth of life."

Musically, Womack is striving for something complex and improbable but nonetheless quintessentially local: homage to the magnificent land that grounds and surrounds the people of Hawai'i. But will an audience of local people respond positively to what is admittedly experimental? Hawaiian music chauvinists might argue that he is stretching local traditions too far. Classical purists could claim it doesn't qualify as symphonic music at all. It doesn't really matter. Womack proceeds.

Now, half a year after starting his composition and ten minutes into its thirteen-minute musical odyssey, the moment of truth has arrived. Womack moves down from the balcony and stands near stage left as he has been instructed to do by the symphony's management. Maestro Wong leads the orchestra through the closing moments of "Frozen Fire." During these last seconds, Donald is feeling everything from jubilation to despair. Womack seems to become the poem he has written to accompany his music:

This once fire lies silent.
Restlessly still.
Heat seeps from its pores.
Whispers. Echoes of its return.
In a different time.

Strange how I may stand here
and listen to its harsh beauty.
But only now.
Indifferent time.

Strange that I should stand here
in this place born many times of death.
On fields of frozen fire.

The last note of "Frozen Fire" is played. The silence in the hall seems desperate. Suddenly, a thunderous applause erupts along with a chorus of "bravos." The appreciation and admiration is heartfelt and overwhelming. Maestro Wong beckons Donald to come out on the stage. He is wearing tan pants and an old blue blazer. Presented with flower leis by well-wishers, Womack blinks shyly like an emerging groundhog as 2,000 people spring to their feet and give him a standing ovation. Anna beams with pride, and the next day the music reviewer for the *Honolulu Advertiser* writes a review that ends, "Congratulations, Mr. Womack, on a fine work!"

It is all part of the island way, of course. For thousands of years the land and the people of Hawai'i have been nourished by small experiments. Things cultural no less than natural find a niche and then swirl and mix with other creations to make new sights and sounds. And very soon they come to "fit" and it is as if they had always been around and we just forgot to notice them.

13

Flashing Paddles

When the excavators of the Ala Wai Canal dropped their picks and shovels into the soil of the place called "spouting waters" back in 1919, most of them thought they were building a drainage system for what is now modern Waikīkī. Few of them could have imagined the traditional uses that a man-made channel would be put to seventy-five years later. Or how deeply that particular stretch of water might affect the lives of thousands of Honolulu teenagers.

Early on a Saturday morning, well before sunup, thirty of these adolescents drift in from a nearby parking lot and assemble under the spreading branches of a *hau* tree next to the canal. Moving at a pace that is somewhere between slow motion and no motion, the kids exchange monosyllabic grunts that sound something like "yo" and "hey" and "mmm" when they see each other. In the language of American teenagers, these mutterings are code for "hello," "good morning," "nothing new," "I'm fine," and "how are you?"

Which is about as good linguistically as it will get for awhile. After all, it is 5:45 A.M. and most sensible people, adult or teen, are still asleep. But this group is not especially sensible. To the contrary. Despite the hour and their sleepiness, they are singularly, fervently, and monomanically fixated on one thing: Hawaiian canoe paddling.

One of these kids is Dana Adler, my 16-year-old daughter. Skinny, quiet, tending toward shyness, Dana usually gravitates toward situations where she can melt into the background. But not here. Not when it comes to steering a six-person, forty-foot, 400-pound outrigger canoe. Dana is crazed for all this. She loves the canoes, her crew, her coach, and the lore of the Hawaiian canoe. Most of all, and regardless of whether they win or lose, she loves racing her boat flat out against rival crews from her own and other schools.

Dana isn't too different from the other twenty-nine drowsy kids that have turned out for practice on this particular Saturday. Their team is called "Pac-Five," which is an amalgam of several small high schools including the University of Hawai'i's Laboratory School, La Pietra Hawai'i School for Girls, and Hawai'i Baptist Academy. In Hawai'i, says *kanaka maoli* leader Tom Kaulukukui, where you go (or went) to school is important. It is a kind of tribal affiliation that conveys what valley you grew up in, who your family and peers are, where your loyalties lie, and what people can expect from you. By themselves, none of these tiny institutions could achieve the critical mass needed for full varsity and junior-varsity crews. Combined, they are able to take on the big powerhouse teams of Punahou, Kamehameha, and Mid-Pacific Institute. These are the schools to beat!

So each Saturday, Dana and the rest of the Pac-Five kids come down to the Ala Wai to drill under the tutelage of their coach, Sam Ahai. To my eyes, Sam is a man of heroic proportions. Ever so gently this soft-spoken postal worker takes a group of sullen, lazy, and occasionally obstreperous teenagers, gets them out of bed on a weekend (voluntarily, no less), works them mercilessly, leaves them exhausted, and inspires in them an incredible love of the water. It is an amazing feat, accomplished always with deep respect for the ocean, the kids, and the traditions and rituals of the sport.

Which is very much Sam's way. In addition to being *kanaka maoli,* Sam is also a 51-year-old native son of the Ala Wai area. This area is his home. He grew up on the water just a few blocks away from where the Ilikai Hotel now stands. Even so, his own love affair with paddling didn't start until he was in his 20s. As Sam tells it, a friend invited him to go paddling one afternoon just after he had returned home from a stint in the army. Two weeks later he was crewing in the infamous Moloka'i-O'ahu channel race.

"Seems like I've been coming down here to the Ala Wai Canal all my life," sighs Sam. Even as he says this, Coach Ahai is mobilizing thirty kids, getting them matched up with thirty paddles and then sorted into the right five boats. Some mornings he has the Pac-Fivers run laps, but because this is the last practice before the final race of the season, he wants as much boat time as possible. The kids will paddle 1.5 miles up the Ala Wai against the current and then sprint 1.5 back. They will do this over and over again for hours and by midmorning they will be completely drained.

The key to paddling, however, is not strength. Strength is necessary, but insufficient. Everyone has to paddle hard, but teamwork and spirit are even more important. Seat no. 1, for example, must keep the rhythm. Seat no. 2 calls changes. Seats nos. 3 and 4 are the engines, powering the boat and giving it muscle. Seat no. 5 is safety officer. When the boat flips over (which happens easily), no. 5 counts heads and retrieves paddles. No. 6 is the steersman. He (or in this case, she) must pilot the canoe and make strategic course decisions.

Practicing their jobs, learning to take care of each other, understanding the traditions of the canoe (most of which trace back fifteen centuries and more), and exercising deep respect for the power of the ocean are all part of what Sam teaches. These values also explain why canoe racing is the fastest growing sport in the Islands, and not just in Hawai'i's high schools. Statewide, more than 10,000 paddlers are now organized into eighty clubs and two major statewide associations. At almost any time of the year, canoe-racing events for novices, masters, seniors, women, children, or teens will be in progress somewhere in Hawai'i and in places as far away as Anchorage and Australia.

At the end of this particular practice, the kids lift their boats out of the water, store them bottom side up on racks padded with tires, and wash down their equipment. Then Sam talks with them briefly. No big lecture here. No long list of dos and don'ts. With his quiet voice and powerful presence, he simply reminds them that they have trained hard and that, win or lose, they must do the best they can against the more-powerful private school teams.

On race day the following Tuesday, dozens of teen-girl paddler crews from high schools around the city congregate at Magic Island across from Ala Moana Shopping Center. The atmosphere is festive. Parents and friends mill around with cameras. Curious visitors pour out of nearby hotels and converge with the local gawkers into a large knot of humanity. Coaches huddle with race officials. Some kids go through warm-ups. Others check their equipment or stand around with teammates and talk strategy. Several tall, powerful-looking teen-girl paddlers who could pass for Olympians have brought along their teddy bears.

Most of the crews from the big schools like Punahou and Kamehameha have state-of-the-art equipment. They are wearing singlets and shorts that match the colors of their schools and their boats. With great fanfare, each school carries its canoe down to the water. Kamehameha High School goes first. Then Punahou, Mid-Pacific Institute, and St. Francis. Finally, there is Pac-Five. The Pac-Five girls are the Cinderellas of this competition, a cobbled-together team. They are using borrowed and slightly beat-up canoes. Nonetheless, they carry themselves with great dignity and enthusiasm and sport their own Pac-Five T-shirts.

In canoeing, as in other local high school sports, rivalries tend to be fierce but not unfriendly. Honolulu is a very small town. Most kids have friends and relatives on other teams. Before the race starts the teams swirl, mingle, and blend as the girls visit with each other and exchange good-natured boasts. In Hawai'i, these attachments will last a lifetime. Canoe racing accentuates the camaraderie and deepens the bonds that are being forged. But it does something else as well.

As race time approaches, the kids paddle their boats out to the starting positions in the mouth of the channel. The varsity teams go first, followed by the junior varsity. The canoes line up and hold their positions in the waves and then, at the first blast from the race official's foghorn, the Varsity-1 crews furiously dig their paddles into the water. Five minutes later, the Varsity-2 teams depart. Then, in short order, the Junior Varsity-1 and Junior Varsity-2 teams take off. Twenty minutes into the race, some fifty canoes are tracing the four-mile course off Waikīkī.

I watch Dana's Junior Varsity-1 boat through binoculars from a promontory point at the outer edge of Magic Island. Through the glasses I see Dana and her crew pulling hard. Arms stretch forward in syncopated rhythm. Backs bend toward the water. Then, steadily and evenly, all six paddlers pull back hard to finish their strokes. They do this repeatedly and relentlessly with good cadence and good movement of the boat through the swells. They seem to be having a good race.

Two minutes later, Dana's canoe becomes indistinguishable from the others around it. Even with high-powered field glasses, I can't tell whose boat is leading. So I walk back to the crowd milling around the finish line. Coach Sam is calmly staring out to sea, waiting. As it is for parents, so it is for coaches. The moment of truth. The letting go. The kids must do this on their own. I stand quietly with Sam, saying nothing, just watching.

The afternoon is glorious, filled with sand, spray, and foam. A gentle, onshore breeze is blowing in our faces. Waves lap the shore and sunlight dapples the water. Across Magic Island swimmers, sailors, board sailors, boogie boarders, and surfers are luxuriating in the warmth of the day. But it is the canoe race that commands the most attention where several hundred people are now lined up waiting for the end.

And then the first canoes start to return. One by one, sleek, low-riding craft with names like *Koa Kai* and *Mālolo* begin to cross the finish line powered by Hawai'i's fine and beautiful young women. Not unexpectedly, the first boats in are the Varsity-1 crews from Kamehameha and Punahou, which arrive neck and neck. Then come the Varsity-1 and 2 crews from Mid-Pacific Institute and the other schools and, right behind them, several Junior Varsity boats, including Dana's. Dana and her crew are deliriously happy. They have not won their heat, but they have placed. More important to them, they have caught up with and ultimately beat their own varsity team, which will be a point of bragging and good-natured teasing of the seniors for weeks to come.

As Dana's crew brings their boat ashore, the kids raise their paddles in a show of victory. They beach their canoe, give themselves a group hug, and then immediately disperse into a huge mass of girls who are congratulating each other and chattering about the race and its defining moments.

Quietly surveying the entire scene from the sideline is Sam Ahai. As he stands there, arms folded, eyes sweeping in everything, the sense of accomplishment he feels for his scrappy little team is obvious. But something bigger is also going on. What Sam knows and will never talk about is the special pride of seeing young people find their *mana,* their inner power. *Mana* has no exact translation into English. It is a unique concept found across the great triangle of water that forms Polynesia, from its westernmost point in New Zealand to its easternmost point on Easter Island to its northern apex here in Hawai'i. *Mana* is sacred. It is all about soul and capacity and moral compass. For Sam, it is days like this that are transformative, when a little girl begins to know that within herself there is a woman warrior.

14

Breakfast in Paradise

It's early morning in America. You have been awake and on the road for several hours and have just entered the rolling hills of southern Wisconsin. Or maybe it's New Hampshire. Or maybe you are crossing the flat, dun-colored wheat fields of central Kansas. Or it could be California, Tennessee, Arizona, or Vermont. It could be anywhere in America. No matter what time zone you happen to live in, the experience is roughly the same. It's a ritual of sorts.

You are driving into a sunrise. Tires thrum on the asphalt as the sun ascends on the eastern horizon. At this hour, your true inner self is emerging and your mind's eye is starting to conceptualize a universe larger and farther-reaching than the driver's side of the car. Specifically, you are thinking: "coffee." Not just sometime soon, but coffee NOW. And not just coffee, but breakfast with it! As the miles peel away and the landscape lengthens, you start having an out-of-body sausage and scrambled egg experience. You see fruit, toast, ham, French toast, oatmeal, dry cereal, sausage, steak, and a side of hash browns.

And after that, more coffee.

So you start looking for a place to eat. Soon enough you find a small town with a little restaurant that is open. You park your car next to a bunch of semis and pickups and walk inside. You look around, sniff the air, and suddenly the morning is transformed by the rich aromas of sizzling bacon and crisp toast, and the lovely sight of two perfect eggs served sunny-side up with a small breakfast steak. You also experience a sudden, overwhelming sense of déjà vu. You've been here before!

Which may just be possible, even though you haven't. What you have just stumbled into is a ubiquitous piece of Americana known as the local cafe. Every community, every neighborhood, and every small town has at least one. These are special institutions, places where communities gather to read the newspaper, meet friends, slurp coffee, fuel up for a hard morning's work, or just shoot the breeze.

The little restaurants I'm talking about are instantly recognizable. They might even be connected by invisible threads. Maybe it's the guy named Bill who owns it. Or Slim, the short-order cook, who is flipping slabs of French toast on the griddle. It might be the waitress who calls you "Hon" or just maybe it's the food itself: baking powder biscuits, big as cannonballs, and served fresh out of the oven with honey or blackberry jam; golden pancakes the size of hubcaps; omelettes that could stoke the boilers of a battleship or power up a forklift.

This place might be a favorite truck stop near Tuba City, Arizona, or a joint called "Ben's" in the middle of New York City. It might be a small inn near Bar Harbor, Maine, or a little one-room place in downtown Quincy, Illinois. Wherever it is, you can bet that the coffee will be strong, the conversations will be interesting, and the food will fill you up.

Twenty-five hundred miles out across the Pacific Ocean, Hawai'i has its own versions of the universal "local cafe." Actually, we have several of them. Some are traditional meat-and-potatoes eateries. They serve the everyday, garden-variety stuff that local people have been enjoying in the Islands for generations. Others infuse some of the new Hawaiian cuisine into their menus by weaving together flavorful ingredients that startle the brain and please the taste buds.

New or old, breakfast in paradise has one thing in common: it is a cross-cultural and cross-culinary encounter. Take the little place in my neighborhood called "Fresh Market." Fresh Market is part of a new breed of microrestaurants that are doing a brisk breakfast trade in their home communities. It seats about thirty people and gathers a broad cross section of early morning patrons. The incongruous regulars who come in every day include a gaggle of house painters and contractors, some professors from the university, a couple of dentists, and two women who jog down the valley with their beagles after the sun is up.

The food at Fresh Market is tasty, but most of it isn't unique. They serve crepes, bagels, and Belgian waffles along with your usual assortment of muffins, scones, and croissants. But nestled well into the interior of their menu is something called Okinawan sweet potato pancakes. Crisply fried on the outside, purple and sweet on the inside, this pancake is strangely delicious, especially when it is accompanied by a papaya-pineapple-*liliko'i* fruit smoothie or some hibiscus ginger tea.

Other nouveau-Hawaiian cafes offer similar, upscale fare, things like chocolate-cinnamon French toast made with Punalu'u Portuguese sweet bread, Hawaiian frittatas, *poke* omelettes that are stuffed with chunks of fresh fish spiced with green onion, and fluffy stacks of macadamia pancakes surrounded by exotic local fruits. All of which is fine and dandy if your tastes run beyond the ordinary. For those seeking something more basic and stick-to-the-ribs, you have to go to breakfast joints that have been around for awhile.

Columbia Inn (downtown, next to the newspaper building) qualifies as one of those. Founded in 1941, it venerates the three things local people love the most: sports, politics, and "talking story." Food is actually a bit secondary here. It's the mingling and palavering that counts. Hence the general hubbub of a hundred or so people who are eating breakfast, stopping at other tables to gab, and pronouncing loudly about who should and shouldn't be running for public office and why.

At Columbia Inn, people do all of these things simultaneously. They park themselves under the framed jerseys of local football greats Jessie Sapolu and Al Noga and adjudicate the errors of the referee at last night's basketball game. They sit in the gray bleacher chairs salvaged from the old Honolulu Stadium (known with great affection as "The Termite Palace") and read the *Hawai'i Hochi,* the *Honolulu Advertiser,* and the *Korea Times.* They eavesdrop on the conversations of politicians holding court with their advisers and nod good morning to the Chinese, Japanese, and Hawaiian families that have been coming there at least once a week for the last decade.

Mind you, you will also see people eating. Young and old, large and small, asleep or awake, everyone will be chowing down piles of fried rice, beef stew, and all-you-can-eat pancakes. Many go straight for the loco moco, a breakfast delicacy invented in Hilo and dispassionately composed of steamed rice, a large hamburger patty, homemade gravy, and a fried egg on top. In lieu of the traditional strips of bacon and slices of ham, some people will have grilled *mahimahi,* Portuguese sausage, or corned beef hash with it. A few larger gentlemen will have all three. For the faint of heart, however, there is always a bran muffin, which the Columbia Inn staff will serve you if you insist on such frugalities.

But even as the Columbia Inn's dexterous wait staff thread their way through the morning conclaves with coffee refills, an entirely different breakfast is unfolding in the industrial part of town at Ethel's Grill on Kalihi Street. If you are a serious breakfast eater, Ryoko Ishii, owner and manager, will fix you up with a meal that will make you shun food for the next two days. Not only that, it will be delicious, cheap, and completely unpretentious. Ethel's is the place where famous chefs like Sam Choy go when they want to eat out.

But first you have to find your way in. More than likely you will have a hard time locating parking. If you are lucky, you may discover a spot down the street near R. M. Nakamura's plumbing company or at Masa's Foreign Car Service. Then, threading your way between the double-parked trucks from Higa's Meat Market and Aloha Gas, you will have to get a table. Which might be a problem because Ethel's Grill only has a few of them and they are almost always filled.

But finally, after the handsome Samoan family of five has finished breakfast, after the two smiling Hawaiian and Chinese businessmen have left, and after the four big workers from the Board of Water Supply have moved their table to make some room, you will squeeze in and order. If you eat what the others are having, you will order a jumbo bowl of miso noodles, some wonton *min,* or what looks like a small washtub full of oxtail soup. Or, if you are feeling like something more traditional, you'll order bacon and eggs. My advice is to order fish because the *mahimahi, akule,* and *'ahi* are always fresh.

While you wait, you should also look around and study this place with some care. Pictures of famous sumo wrestlers adorn the wall along with a calendar from Redline Automotive. Two burly drivers from the Touchdown Trucking Company will probably come in, say hello to Ryoko and her kitchen help, and settle themselves in with the guys from the Board of Water Supply. Meanwhile, a couple of ants will be walking across the wall and there's some dust balls on the floor, but you will be the only person who notices these things and my advice is to pay them no mind.

While everyone else is quietly concentrating on eating, the food will come. And the food will keep coming! Ryoko herself is a woman of few words. Soon enough she will silently start to bring things to your table. Mind you, it is 6:30 A.M. First it's a fresh salad with light Italian dressing. Next, some coffee. Then she delivers up a big bowl of rice followed by a tangle of crisp bacon over a mountain of eggs with green onions stirred in. Finally, as your meal draws to a close, she will bring out a plate of fresh, raw tuna on a bed of cabbage and served with watercress and pickled garlic.

Here, in Hawai'i's counterpart to the "All-American Breakfast Place," you will feast on a home-cooked breakfast served by a diminutive woman named Ryoko who is known and loved by people from all walks of life. Eventually, of course, she will bring you the bill. It will come to $3.90. It will be delivered with a shy smile and a wish that you will come back again very soon. Which you undoubtedly will when the urge for some customary, everyday, and very good food comes over you and you crave the amalgam of a truly local island cafe.

15

Passage

One of the most visited spots in Hawai'i is Hanauma Bay, a breathtaking little inlet on the easternmost perimeter of the island of O'ahu. Protected on three sides by steep cliffs and, on the fourth, by a wide fringing reef, Hanauma is a "lagoon paradigm," a kind of universal mental model of what a little cove on a tropical island should look like.

If you want to see this archetype, drive a few miles east out of Honolulu proper and you eventually run right into it. Not coincidentally, it will be at the exact place where between the hours of 9 A.M. and 5 P.M. you will find (and then probably join) a long line of cars snaking down a steep hill into the lovely beach park and marine conservation district at the bottom. You will park your car and then descend on the old road and footpath that leads to the beach itself.

Because it is a marine sanctuary, Hanauma Bay exerts a palpable gravitational pull. It is one of those spots that people dream of. Hanauma is all about underwater adventure, which is available to young and old just a few feet from shore. Stick a snorkel and mask on your head, wade into the shallows, poke your face in the water, and the richness and diversity of Hawai'i's ocean immediately unfolds. Suddenly, you are eyeball-to-eyeball with a reticulated butterfly fish, a Moorish idol, a school of convict tangs, a black-speckled moray eel, a family of sand-hugging bonefish, a green sea turtle, a cloud of gray mullets, a fast-moving blue crevally, and a dozen large parrotfish munching pieces of a coral head.

Indisputably, Hanauma Bay is worth seeing if you are smitten with the idea of swimming with tropical fish. The downside, of course, is that you are also going to be with a lot of other people. Everyone else in the world will also be there jostling for a piece of sand to spread a towel on or paddling around the same spiny puffer fish that you just happen to be scrutinizing through your mask. That's why some of us who live here very rarely go to Hanauma Bay by the conventional method. Instead, we approach the bay on foot, from above, and from afar. It's a pilgrimage of sorts, with slightly different aspirations and motives.

It all started one Sunday morning nearly fifteen years ago when a group of us, all close friends, drove out to the cliff area above Hanauma to see the sunrise. It was just a nice thing to do, a pleasant weekend diversion organized by John Barkai, but that particular hike started a tradition that continues to this day. In the predawn light John, Linda, Elizabeth, Kent, Kem, Junko, Carolyn, and I parked our cars about a mile away from the bay and ascended Koko Head, the large crumbling tuff cone that rises up to form the bay's backdrop.

Koko Head takes its name from a small canoe landing that once existed in the area. "Koko" means blood, and the surrounding area, which includes another equally eroded volcanic feature called Koko Crater, is named for the earth that, in ancient times, turned crimson when a man was bitten by a mythic shark. The ocher-colored ground of Koko Head is a fine example of volcanic weathering. On its western side, much of the old tuff cone has been washed away by centuries of rainfall, leaving behind long cuts and gullies, some more than forty feet deep. On the other side, Koko Head is relentlessly attacked by wind and waves. The result: spectacular 300-foot cliffs, deep furrows and notches, a honeycomb of sea caves, and a rich plant and animal life that most people never see.

That particular morning was cool and windy. We walked up the baked red earth via the old jeep road that runs along the spine of the ridge and stops at the top near several small, fenced buildings containing air traffic tracking equipment. The hike wasn't long, nor was it particularly strenuous, although it did take us up and over a thousand-foot rise. Nonetheless, we took it at a slow, almost lazy pace, savoring the sweet morning air, the broad panoramic views of Moloka‘i, Maui, and Lāna‘i, and the windswept solitude that permeates the cliffs and reminds you that you are nearly 2,500 miles from anyplace else.

The weather was perfect, and it held. We arrived at the top in time to pour some steaming coffee from a thermos and settle down on some rocks to watch the sunrise. Looking due east we saw the colors of the sky transform from a deep ink black, to an eggplant purple, to the colors of honey and amber. We saw the last stars blink out and the orb of the sun erupt like a great orange and yellow ball bobbing to the surface on the sea's farther horizon. Then slowly, when the sun was higher, we watched the sky turn sharp and crystalline like the blue of a robin's egg.

But our day was just starting. In that fresh dawn, we sipped coffee, ate fruit and new baked bread, and then descended Koko Head's eastern side, just opposite of where we had come up. Our intent was to explore two small craters on Koko Head's flanks, one called ‘Ihi‘ihilauākea, named for the nearly extinct wide-leaved *‘ihi‘ihi* fern that is found in that spot and nowhere else, and the other called Nonoʻula (lit., "red sunburn"). The hike took us over a crusty, exposed hardpan, through clumps of fountain grass, and down to the ocean's edge.

There, at the outermost point on the right side of Hanauma Bay, at that specific place the old Hawaiians called Paiʻoluʻolu Point (meaning "lifted gently"), we noticed them. Whales. A large pod of humpbacks, rising, spouting, and cartwheeling through the surf, then sounding just offshore in the swirling blue-green waters. We stood, mesmerized by the flashing flukes, the long white flippers, and the plumes of water bursting from their blowholes. And when they were gone, we reminded ourselves that these particular whales are part of that small and specific northern humpback population that annually migrates between Hawaiʻi and the Arctic each year to give birth to its young.

We saw other old friends and winter visitors from the Arctic as well. Petrels, shearwaters, and frigatebirds wheeled and soared offshore. Beneath them, green sea turtles paddled through the swells and combers. In and around the rocks we found beach heliotrope, prickly poppy, and small, tough *kiawe* trees permanently bent before the wind. Hiking into ʻIhiʻihilauākea, we eventually found the stand of rare, broad-leaved ferns and, in their midst, a golden-plover in its black-breasted summer plumage squawking as it defended its little territory by rushing at other intruding birds. Like the humpback whales, the plover is a part-time resident, summering in the Arctic, wintering in the Islands.

Later in the morning, we hiked back up to the old jeep road at the top of the crater and then made our way back to the cars. That particular day—hot, sweaty, but full of energy—we joined the throngs visiting Hanauma Bay. We donned masks, flippers, and snorkels; paddled out over the reef into deeper water; saw barracuda, spotted eagle rays, and baby sharks; had lunch; and then departed for home in the early afternoon.

Since that time, our journey to the eroding cliffs above Hanauma Bay has become a regular event, something we do at least once a year, and some years twice. Most years we go in the spring to see the passage of the whales through the Moloka'i Channel or on a cooler winter morning in December when rain squalls lash O'ahu. Some years, we go on Easter or Labor Day for a special sunrise and we bring along a few other acquaintances and out-of-town visitors. But mostly it is our little core group that goes back year after year, regular as rain, steady as a heartbeat, predictable as the day that follows night.

When we go, we still bring coffee, fruit, and pastries, and, yes, most years we still grumble about the crowds down at Hanauma Bay and then stop there for a swim anyway. There are changes, of course. Some of our group have moved away from Hawai'i and new friends have joined us. More recently, we notice that our teenage kids now ascend the old jeep road a little faster than we do and we joke about a new disease we recently discovered and call "leviathitis" or "whale anxiety," your basic fear of not seeing what everyone else seems to be pointing at out on the salt.

But we all know that the rite of ascending Koko Head needs to be honored. Why? It is the allure of the island in all of us, that same inner pattern that compels us to explore any remote and lonely place. Standing above Hanauma Bay, we point our faces into the wind and feel the sense of wholeness that always comes from standing at the center of a long, circular horizon. Then the exquisiteness of the moment pours into us. We become a part of the red earth, the blusterous landscape, the pods of whales, and the squawking seabirds. We intersect with their complex passages and mark our own circles of friendship to remind ourselves of our roots and this place we call home.

16

Garden Fever

All in and out among the blooms,
A gray and graceful palm-tree looms
Above the flower beds. Its fronds
Are mirrored in my lily ponds.

So wrote Don Blanding in a little book of doggerel called
Leaves from a Grass House published in 1923. Blanding, unofficial poet laureate of the Islands, loved Hawaiian gardens and proclaimed his herbal affections repeatedly.
Trees captivated him. Shrubs sent shivers of jubilation vibrating through his poems. Tropical flowers made him swoon. All
of it became the stuff of his verses.

Luckily for Blanding, he never hung out at my house or with
my friends and in-laws. If he did, I suspect he would be writing
about gardening psychosis and the strange compulsions that
accompany flower and vegetable planting. With landscapes
and microenvironments that range from desert to rain forest
and even to areas that are truly alpine, Hawai'i is a perfect place

to grow things. And these days just about everyone I know in Hawaiʻi is going botanically berserk.

The place to begin is my house. Each year about this time Carolyn and I get it into our heads to spruce up a certain little patch of dirt in the corner of the yard called "Pet Cemetery." The name comes from a long line of goldfish, guinea pigs, and canaries that have gone to their final reward and now rest in well-fertilized peace. I keep telling her we should grow papayas and squash there, but Carolyn will have none of it. It's flowers she wants, especially *pīkake. Pīkake* is a member of the jasmine family, and Carolyn loves them dearly. "Food is OK," she says, "but flowers are for the soul."

So each year, trowels and hoes in hand, we trudge outside and try to grow the fragrant white blossoms she prizes so much. We work valiantly to resuscitate the plumerias, violets, and gingers that are clinging to life despite our previous year's abuse. We plant, trim, water, and offer soothing words of encouragement to each plant. But our annual efforts always come to naught. Ants and slugs attack the spider lilies. Cats and dogs scratch up the gardenias. The plumeria gets root rot and swarms of whiteflies gobble up the bananas. And the viney *pīkake,* which everyone says is easy to grow? It sinks roots, throws up branches, sends out endless runners, spreads its biomass around, but produces nary a flower.

My in-laws on the windward side of the island have a different kind of problem. KC and Gail Watanabe, their two teenage sons Reid and Bryce, and Gail's mom, Grandma Ruth, all live at a place called Kokokahi. It's cool and wet there and a bit like the little plantation town of Hāwī on the Big Island where Gail and Ruth grew up.

Unlike Carolyn and I who are gardening-disabled, Gail and Ruth have transformed the swales and gullies of their backyard into a small paradise. Their garden is filled with tree ferns, anthuriums, white gingers, impatiens, heleconias, orchids, and various fruit trees set off ever so artfully by an emerald patch of mondo grass through which runs a white stone walkway. It is cool, inviting, and tasteful.

But all this inspired beauty has a dark side. It is fueled by slave labor. Ken, Bryce, and Reid are regularly conscripted to rake leaves, mow lawns, and trim hedges. As it turns out, that's the easy stuff. Every once in a while, Gail raises her left eyebrow, gives the three men a menacing look, and points to the yard. The guys immediately turn off the basketball game and dutifully march out into the yard looking like basset hounds. It's weeding they hate.

Things are just as odd down the street at my other brother-in-law's house. For years, Brent Watanabe went to elaborate lengths to avoid all forms of yard work. Faced with the inevitable problems that shedding trees and growing grass bring to home ownership, his attitude was "cement them over." Basically, he was a Darwinian who preferred to let the winners and losers sort themselves out while he noodled around with his computer.

Today, he is a thoroughly transformed man, a born-again gardener whose newly acquired belief system centers on native Hawaiian plants. This late-blooming interest was instigated by my niece Erin, who is a student of hula. Done in the traditional form, hula requires the use of certain indigenous plants that are worn as clothing and placed on altars. Rather than buying them, Brent and his wife Julie, parsimonious folks that they are, decided to grow them. Their yard is now overflowing with ti, *'ōhi'a, hāpu'u, hala, 'ilima, kukui,* hibiscus, and other lovely plants that are native to the Islands.

But where the garden has flourished, Brent and Julie have gone into a noticeable decline. These formerly fun-loving and gregarious souls are now "yard addicts" who toil their weekends and vacations away doing horticulture instead of hedonistically relishing life like they used to. Gone are Saturday night movies, eating out, and the wicked little Sunday Scrabble tournaments with family and friends. Instead, life is a steady round of fertilizers, plant sales, and watering schedules.

Brent is not the only one who is trying to scratch the big gardening itch. My pal Ellen Carson is spending major parts of her life babying a couple of key lime trees at her place overlooking Kāne'ohe Bay. Russell Kokubun, using his pet pig Willy-Boy as a rototilling machine, is fanatically trying to raise pumpkins. And here in Mānoa Valley, the ever-patient Louie Chang is spending weekends introspectively hunkered over his herb garden watching his lemon grass, Thai basil, and Chinese parsley grow.

For a truly fine form of gardening mania, however, meet Brad Coates, lawyer, author, ocean kayaker, marathon runner, theater lover, opera afficionado, and world traveler (118 countries). Brad is a man who lives life on a grand scale and loves pageantry. He and his lovely wife Sachi live on a 10,000-foot lot on the slopes of 'Āina Haina Valley. From street level on Kulu'iPlace, Brad and Sachi's home looks more or less normal, but the plastic Santa Claus is best taken as a sign of things to come.

"There's an old Chinese proverb," explains Brad, "that says if you want to be happy for a night, get drunk. If you want to be happy for a year, get married. And if you want to be happy for life, grow a garden." On that theory, the Coates garden begins just outside the door of their lānai. It ascends to the top of the hill as a series of meandering pathways, flower patches, terraces, gazebos, and outdoor sitting areas. Because 'Āina Haina is hot, Brad has planted agave, cactus, yucca, bottle and sego palms, various species of cacti, and bougainvillea, all of which require very little water. He has also built an aviary and is raising lovebirds, cockatoos, and parakeets.

By themselves, the little plant communities that Brad has established on the side of 'Āina Haina Valley are nice examples of xeriscaping. In pockets of cinders and soil he has planted bromeliads and cactus that now and then produce stunning red, orange, and white blossoms that rise up to meet the sun on long, slender stalks. Some reach for the moon and only bloom at night.

But Brad's desert-loving herbage is just a backdrop for the real garden, which consists of certain strategically placed garden ornaments. Interspersed between the palms and nestled amongst the aloes are plastic dinosaurs, pink flamingos, cement frogs, ceramic rabbits, and broken surfboards planted upright like tombstones. There is a New Mexico "Extra Terrestrial Highway" license plate hanging from a *koa* tree and an old bowling trophy sitting on a rock. Six oversized salad forks have been painted in bright colors and strung like tinsel from the limb of a fig tree. And at the top of the hill, with a view of the entire spread, Brad has positioned an old commode with a pineapple plant growing out of it.

Toiletry aside, most of Brad's garden-o-bilia comes from his travels. "Brad is a collector," says Sachi, "but his standard of collecting is a bit different." To qualify for the garden, says Brad, an item can't cost more than thirty dollars and needs to be weatherproof. "And," he adds with a chuckle, "if the neighbors ever catch up with me, it probably ought to be bulletproof."

As Brad tours me through the garden he meticulously explains the origins of certain masks that are attached to trees and a five-foot bronze horse that is trying to gallop across a patch of grass. He shows me a pile of new stuff that he just brought back from Chile and a piece of Indonesian glass that is sitting on the deck outside his kitchen. "Basically," he explains, "I ran out of room for all this junk inside the house and started putting it in the garden."

Brad and Sachi spend a good amount of time maintaining their yard, but there is also an annual focal point in which yard, house, and assorted humans all come together in a giant extravaganza. Each year on their anniversary Brad and Sachi throw a massive garden party and several hundred friends and associates show up at "Casa de Coates" to eat, drink, hang out in the garden, and watch the sunset. Typical of any other local get-together, everyone contributes food or drink to the gala and a few people will even bring a curio that they picked up at the Goodwill Store.

The next day, of course, Brad will wake up a little later than usual and start cleaning. He will straighten up his "hula dog," which combines a toy mutt with a mannequin in a grass skirt, place the grinning ceramic pig that somebody gave him in the shade of a monstera plant, and gather the leftover paper plates, cups, and soda cans. Then he will do what he loves the most, which is watering his plants and pottering about with the odd toys that make the entire Coates enterprise so bright and inviting.

While Brad and Sachi are cleaning up from the night before, Carolyn and I will be struggling heroically with our *pīkake* and Gail, Ruth, and the boys will be pulling weeds. Brent and Julie will be spreading 13-13-13 fertilizer on their prize yellow *'ōhi'a,* and Louie will be picking arugula leaves to add to his salad. And looking down from his garden in the sky, Don Blanding will probably be laughing and reciting the rest of the last verse of his poem called "My Hawaiian Garden," which ends:

When you are passing will you pause
Or—if you will—drop in and see
This garden that belongs to me?

17

Oblivion

On March 1, 1995, 24-year-old Darcy Wilcox, a wilderness afficionado and daughter of two other wilderness afficionados, Carol and Gaylord Wilcox, trekked into the Mōhihi area near Kōkeʻe State Park on the island of Kauaʻi. Like her parents, Darcy is an experienced hiker and camper. Her intention was to cross a long and broad marshy area near Mōhihi, locate an old Hawaiian *heiau* reputed to be near Mount Waiʻaleʻale, camp overnight, and return the next morning. For someone in good shape and knowledgeable about Hawaiʻi's mountains and forests, it all seemed imminently do-able.

True to plan, Darcy made her way across a number of bogs and gulches, found the ruins she was looking for, and spent the night deep in the wilderness. The following morning she started back but took a wrong turn on what turned out to be an old pig trail. Clambering through dense underbrush and circling back on her own trail, Darcy finally realized she was lost. Then, she did what experienced hikers are supposed to do: find a clearing, set up camp, sit tight.

Seven days after entering the swamp, Darcy was found thanks to an extensive ground and air search launched by Gaylord and Carol and local rescue teams. She was hungry, thirsty, and tired but unhurt. For Darcy, it was a happy ending. Others haven't been as fortunate. In 1990 a young couple on vacation, one a postgraduate student, the other a Harvard researcher, set off to explore the same locale Darcy had hiked through. The two were never seen or heard from again.

The area that disoriented Darcy, and that has confused many others, is called the Alaka'i Swamp. It is a treacherous place, not to be taken lightly. If I was a cartographer rendering a likeness of Kaua'i, my depiction would look like one of those tenth-century European maps that were made when people knew that the world was flat. On my version of Kaua'i, there would be a few central chunks of terra firma that have long Hawaiian names and, farther out and toward the north, increasing amounts of blank space. Beyond that, after skirting an area I would call The Edge of Nothingness, I would have you come to a place called Oblivion with a notation that says: "Here there be Monsters." This is where I would position the Alaka'i Swamp.

On contemporary maps, Alaka'i Swamp is actually a small but not insignificant feature. Look in the north-central section on Kaua'i and you will find it marked off as a splotch of blue and green. Topographic lines indicate that the swamp is above 2,800 feet in elevation. The tight lines on the edges of the swamp show that it is bounded on three sides by cliffs. The blue squiggles that look like tufts of hair suggest that the place is probably on the damp side. What you can't see, however, is how twisted, isolated, interesting, and dangerous this landscape actually is. Maps don't have symbols for these things.

The answer, then, is to see the swamp firsthand, which is exactly what nine of us are doing. We are also encountering monsters. Four of them, to be precise, all standing in front of me. These particular swamp creatures are teenagers, three of them female. Closer up, I can see that the Girl-Things are Adlers: Kelly, Corey, and Dana. The other one is a smiling, blond-haired, blue-eyed boy-apparition named Kent Preiss-Davis, better known as "P.D."

All four of these kids are sweet, wonderful children, but I also smell a rat. Not being able to see their hands makes me nervous. So too do their smiles, which are entirely too nice. The honey-coated "Hi, Daddy" from Kelly, my youngest, gives it all away. I look at them; they look at me. The attack begins at point-blank range.

All four of them hurl large, dripping mud bombs at me. I stoop down, grab my own handful, return a weak and ineffectual volley, and then start to retreat. Rescue comes in the nick of time. P.D.'s folks, Kent and Elizabeth, come charging over from one direction and our friends John, Linda, and Kem from another. Suddenly, viscous strands and globules of mud are being chucked in all directions. Flying mud fills the air.

Then, a dastardly deed occurs. Carolyn, my loyal partner of twenty-eight years, defies the international conventions that govern wars between kids and grownups and joins the youngsters. Amidst squeals and spatters, there is more side switching. Then, others turn coat. What started out as a nice, if slightly lopsided, duel dissolves into an all-out melee full of feints and double crosses. Slowly, all eleven of us are encrusted with another layer of ooze.

Not that a mere mud fight matters very much at this point. Since early morning we have had several such skirmishes and a variety of other full-fury mud wars as we make our way across one of the Alaka'i Swamp's few trails. Our destination is Kilohana Overlook, which is trail's end and which will command a spectacular vista of this part of Kaua'i. The hike is eleven miles round trip. It is not especially steep, but it is long, wet, and exceedingly sloppy. One of my kids is already referring to it as "Dad's Death March."

For several years now, our little gaggle of family and friends has been enjoying brief getaways together around the Islands. This one has us staying in some wooden cabins at a camp near Po'ipū and taking day trips to different spots on the island. Long walks, swimming, boogie boarding, and excursions to remote places like Alaka'i Swamp are all part of the trip. The swamp hike in particular is an expedition that several of us have wanted to do for many years.

Much of the fascination centers on the peculiar terrain. Alaka'i Swamp is situated just above the arid, ten-mile-long, 3,657-feet-deep Waimea Canyon and just below 5,080-foot Mount Wai'ale'ale. Wai'ale'ale, meaning "rippling, overflowing water," is the highest place on Kaua'i and a remnant of the great volcano that originally formed the island. With a measured average annual rainfall of 466 inches, it is one of the wettest places on earth.

Alaka'i gets its own 200-plus inches of rain, which can come down at any time of the year and in any quantity. These tons of water (some of which are falling on us today) collect on the swamp's surface and stay there, creating a seemingly endless and impenetrable bog. Geologically, the Alaka'i is a like a 10,000-acre puddle sitting on an impermeable slab of basalt converted to clay by six million years of wetness. No one lives there permanently. It is mushy terrain. The only visitors are scientists, hikers, pig hunters, and a few *kanaka maoli* who come to gather plants for ceremonies and medicine.

The swamp also holds some of the best stands of native vegetation in Hawai'i. In this extraordinary, seldom-visited habitat, fragrant vines of *maile,* prized by lei makers, twine around the *mokihana* tree, whose fruit exudes an aniselike scent. Lobelias, sedges, mosses, lichens, and the fly-catching sundew plant all can be found here. So too can Hawai'i's rarest birds, including most members of the Hawaiian creeper family and the Kaua'i 'ō'ō, which most consider extinct because it has not been seen since the late 1980s.

For a time, we follow a half-constructed trail of wooden planks and beams set on metal pins pounded into the muck. Sometimes we walk on the beams alone. When the rickety wooden walkway ends, we jump from rock to rock or slosh and wade through a brown muck that has the consistency and viscosity of oatmeal. The terrain we encounter is quiet and mysterious. Cloud forest gives way to small patches of grass and then to deep mires of mud. There is no sun, of course. Just a steamy, dense ground fog that is intermittently broken by drizzle.

Mud—face-splattering, pants-smearing, skin-clinging, personality-changing mud—is a moment-by-moment fact of life in the swamp. Most of the time it is manageable, but once in a while it causes serious consternation. Closing in on Kilohana Overlook with a mile to go, we encounter one of those situations. It happens at a point of weariness when even the teenagers seem to be running out of shenanigans and banter.

All of us are slogging along, brains and legs on automatic pilot. Kent, Linda, and Kem are a hundred feet behind. All of a sudden five-foot, three-inch Linda disappears into what she thinks is solid footing. She is down to her armpits and descending fast. Irritation turns to embarrassment and then to horror. As she sinks, Kent grabs one arm and Kem grabs another. With a long, powerful slurping sound, they extract her from the mud and deposit her on high ground. Lost somewhere in the brown abyss is a prized bracelet.

Linda is the wrong person to have this happen to. Although she is a strong swimmer and an accomplished marathon runner, her concept of a truly great hike is a couple of circuits around a well-appointed shopping mall. There is a bit of good-natured teasing and some jokes about "swamp creatures," but everyone is sobered by what has happened.

Soon enough, we come to Kilohana Overlook, our destination. The overlook commands views that extend from the base of Mt. Wai'ale'ale down through the Wainiha River valley to the sea at Hanalei. We gather on the little wooden platform that marks the spot, but on this day we see nothing. Swamp and valley are completely fogged in with a dense, enigmatic mist. We wait, hoping it will blow over. The fog turns to mist, the mist into rain. After an hour, we leave.

The way back is the way we came, but the return seems shorter. As we get closer to the end, the teenagers get a second wind. Perhaps it is the thought of dry clothes, hot chocolate, and dinner. Encountering other hikers, one of the kids advises them to turn back and bring some flippers. There are more minor mishaps. A ripped raincoat, a lost pocketknife, a sandwich dropped in the mud. Kelly breaks a fingernail on a log and P.D. asks her if she needs a medevac.

Soon enough, we are out of the swamp and walking on a solid trail. For the last mile, we clump our way up an old jeep road. When the rain stops, the muck and ooze that covers us starts to dry. Encrusted and looking slightly mummified, we get back to our parked vehicles in the late afternoon. We scrape off the most egregious layers of Alaka'i mud, fire up the cars, and make our way toward Po'ipū.

Carolyn and the three girls nod off in the back seat as we wind our way down the mountain. We pass through Kōke'e State Park and then drop down through miles and miles of waving sugarcane on the plantations above Waimea. As we approach sea level, I look back in the rearview mirror and catch a glimpse of the forests that edge the Alaka'i's high bogs. And with a shudder, I also see the whites of the eyes of a swamp thing staring back from the glass and following me as we head down from the plateau.

18

Pig Wars

A pig, Ambrose Bierce once opined in the *Devil's Dictionary*, is "an animal closely allied to the human race by the splendor and vivacity of its appetite." On the island of Hawai'i, the "Pig Wars" started when the State of Hawai'i Division of Forestry and Wildlife built two stretches of fence in the Kohala Mountains in the Pu'u o 'Umi Forest Reserve. One fence was intended to protect a sensitive environmental area between two steep cliffs from the feral version of Willy-Boy Kokubun's cousins. The other was part of an intended 1,500-acre endangered plant exclosure.

Both fences deeply alarmed local hunters. Angry complaints were voiced in the press. Letters and phone calls were made to local politicians. Portions of the fence were vandalized and Big Island Forestry and Wildlife employees received death threats. In the United States, most environmental "wars" tend to start this way, with recriminations and threats, with anger and hurt, with escalations into legislative and judicial forums. Once they commence, and once they are politicized, these fights can be filled with invective and unbecoming tactics straight out of Sun Tzu's *Art of War.* But every once in a while, people try something different.

It is late in December. On a wet, cool night very close to Christmas, twenty people are gathered around worn benches and rough plywood tables in the clubhouse of the Laupāhoehoe and Hāmākua Hawaiian Civic Club. Laupāhoehoe is an aging sugar plantation community surrounded by remnant cane fields and, above the cane fields, forest. Hāmākua is the name of the local district. In the town itself, most of the wooden houses are small and have corrugated iron roofs. The clubhouse is slowly returning to the elements, a victim of age and termites. Nonetheless, it is clean and dignified. It is freshly swept and someone has set a vase of newly picked and fragrant gardenias on the front table.

The group that has assembled inside is known as the "NAWG," which is an acronym for Natural Areas Working Group. It includes representatives from three Big Island hunting groups, two local community associations, the Sierra Club Legal Defense Fund, the Audubon Society, the National Biological Survey, and the State of Hawai'i's Division of Forestry and Wildlife. My job, as one of two co-mediators, is to structure a process of communication and negotiation and increase the odds that new solutions to some vexing old problems can be invented. My co-mediator's name is Alice Paet Ah Sing. We have been teamed up by the State of Hawai'i to try and help do some problem solving.

This meeting is the NAWG's fifteenth in eight months, and the specific task is to put the finishing touches on a document that contains fifty recommendations aimed at resolving longstanding controversies between hunters, environmentalists, and state foresters. The presenting issue is the impact of ungulates (hoofed animals) in Hawai'i's forests. Pigs are everywhere in Hawai'i, including my neighborhood in urban Honolulu, but the geographic epicenter of this particular conflict is the 80,000 acres making up the Big Island's Natural Area Reserves (NARs) near Laupāhoehoe, Hilo, and Waimea.

Natural Area Reserves are ecologically important tracts of land that have been set aside by the state, in perpetuity, as prime examples of Hawai'i's extraordinarily diverse environment. There are many different NARs. On O'ahu, one of them preserves a coastal strand replete with ancient sand dunes. There is another on top of 14,000-foot Mauna Kea that flags a good example of Hawai'i's little-known high-altitude tundra. The Mauna Kea reserve is, in fact, the remnant of an ancient glacier. Most reserves, however, seek to sustain and showcase Hawai'i's last native rain forests, which are perceived to be under siege from both natural and unnatural forces, including pigs.

Scientists marshal considerable evidence to show that pigs indiscriminately tear through local plant life, particularly in the rain forests, and pave the way for such other invasive pests as mosquitoes, which carry avian malaria, and the banana poka vine, which chokes out native trees. Pigs like Willy-Boy weigh up to 300 pounds. They are prolific breeders and relentless rooters and cause havoc when left unchecked. A lone pig, say ecologists, can completely denude a large swath of land in a single night. Multiplied manyfold, they present a spreading danger to the forest habitats for Hawai'i's disappearing native creatures. For biologists, the usual remedy is to exterminate them.

Local hunters, most of whom are *kanaka maoli,* hold a very different view. They have vociferously resisted animal eradication and most attempts to remove them from critical bird and plant habitats. They contest much of the scientific evidence presented by environmentalists and assert that pigs are both an organic part of the landscape and an esteemed cultural and recreational resource. They argue further that, during hard times in economically depressed places like Hāmākua on the island of Hawai'i, they are an economic necessity.

For a variety of reasons, therefore, the pig issue greatly rankles many *kanaka maoli.* Wild pigs are traditional food. For many *kanaka maoli,* pigs are very much part of what is deemed to be "natural." In this context, and fueled further by the forces of cultural revitalization, pigs are political and symbolic. *Kanaka maoli* activists are asserting strong claims for independence and reparations from both the state and federal governments. The pig issue adds to this larger debate and involves charges of "eco-imperialism" and a call for *kanaka maoli* dominion over Hawai'i's forests. "Why," says one of the hunters, "should some scientist from America get to come here and tell us that this plant or that bird is more important than us? We will decide these things for ourselves."

Which is precisely what the NAWG and this particular mediation effort is all about.

Staked out in the extreme, the opening mediation positions have a Bosnia-like intractability about them. Some members of the working group advocate putting up as many stretches of pig-proof fences as possible, removing the pigs inside, and, over time, expanding the Natural Area Reserve system so that more forest is protected. Others take a polar-opposite approach. They argue that pig populations and hunting opportunities must be expanded, that some of the NARs should be turned into Game Management Areas, and that all existing fences in and around the NARs need to be torn down because they interfere with pig breeding and migration and are dangerous to hikers, hunters, and dogs.

In general, these early arguments have a certain weariness about them: the posturing produces a great deal of heat but very little light. At times it feels as if everyone is playing out a prechoreographed part. In turn, there is also a pattern whereby the natural ideological differences between these camps are exacerbated by a few "conflict junkies," who approach every difference of opinion as a holy war, a personal duel, a general amusement, or as just one more small chance to display the cranky and obstreperous side of their personality.

Luckily, the NAWG is composed of people who hold very strong opinions but who also genuinely want to solve problems and—in the finest tradition of *hoʻoponopono,* the ancient *kanaka maoli* process of resolving family and clan disputes— seek to "make things right." There is the inevitable stereotyping, miscommunication, misinformation, noninformation, interpersonal irritation, and battles over process that attend any conflict. Most NAWG members, however, seem preliminarily interested in a search for understanding and agreement.

At the first meeting, pleasantries are exchanged, but the underlying mood is dark. People regard one another with suspicion, and everyone eyeballs us mediators because no one quite knows how this process will really work. Then the meeting commences. There are introductions, some perfunctory opening statements, and then we spend two hours negotiating meeting procedures and interpersonal etiquettes. These protocols are extremely important. They provide real rules of engagement, the first tangible agreements, and simple overtures of trust and goodwill.

At the second and third meetings, and throughout subsequent sessions, the group tackles substance. Despite the heated outbursts that occasionally punctuate the discussions, the group pools critical information. Much of our work as mediators is directed at choreographing and moderating the way ideas, knowledge, data, and assumed wisdom are exchanged. Each group has its "filters" for taking in and giving information. The scientists try to be dispassionate in their presentations, which is irksome to the *kanaka maoli,* who see them as aloof. The government officials like to think about problems in terms of regulations and political nuances, which drives the environmentalists crazy. When the Hawaiians and community people speak, they give long, angry, scolding speeches, which irritates the scientists and government people.

These differences in organizational "style" are part of the ambient conditions of the mediation process. Our goal is to help everyone get the questions right, to manage the multiple layers and conflicting crosscurrents of information exchange, and to facilitate mutual interpretation of data so that it produces "usable knowledge." In the process, the group learns practical and immediate tolerance. When one of the environmentalists makes overly sweeping generalizations, other members of her own coalition rope her back to the table. And when one of the hunters presents a completely ungrounded theory of a pig "motherland" and radiating migrations from a certain valley, the rest of the group disagrees with him with respect and forbearance.

Real breakthroughs, however, occur when the NAWG works out a common goal and signs off on a series of guiding statements. These "agreements-in-principle" become the beacons that help navigate the group toward specific solutions. They do not specifically solve the dispute, but they create the contours and parameters within which agreements can be fashioned later on. In this case, the guiding principles move everyone to common ground.

The principles go like this: Conceptually everyone concurs that more forest areas could be specifically administered for hunting, and that these areas could sustain more pigs. Other areas, it is agreed, might be managed in such a way that there are no pigs or the lowest number possible. Everyone acknowledges that local hunters should be the ones to help manage pig numbers by pressuring the pigs out of the high-density areas. Finally, it is agreed that proper forest management is not simply the job of the Division of Forestry and Wildlife. The private and civic sectors and abutting communities need to be involved.

The key to making these agreements work will be joint monitoring and "adaptive management" carried out by a set of newly created local entities called regional forest "Management Advisory Councils" (MACs). Each of the councils will be composed of hunters, scientists, environmental advocates, government foresters, and people from nearby towns. The MACs will help organize joint monitoring projects, volunteer efforts, and local educational programs. Each MAC will also send a representative to sit on a central coordinating committee that, for lack of a better title, is initially identified as the "Big MAC."

Although there are many disagreements on the road to conceptual clarity, the NAWG progressively works through the nuances involved in these agreements. From my point of view, it is gratifying to watch this group of former enemies learn to tolerate and, in some circumstances, actually value differences of opinion. The discussions are still fierce when it comes to content but increasingly they are self-regulating, comfortable, and collegial in style. Each meeting begins and ends with a prayer or chant, sometimes said by a non-Hawaiian. There is humor. People bring food. They mingle at breaks and inquire about each other's families. They bring small gifts for each other. They tell stories. Over time, they begin to see each other in new and different ways. As co-mediators, Alice and I notice these things. Process, politics, and relationships merge together with substance.

As the fifteenth meeting comes to a close, there is a tangible sense of accomplishment among the community members, hunters, scientists, and state foresters who make up the NAWG. Adversaries who at one time would not even be seen publicly with one another have walked in each other's shoes, worked side by side, and produced some breakthrough agreements that may just make a difference. These agreements won't solve every problem, but they are a start, and everyone knows it.

Just as important is the unique chemistry of peacemaking that has been engaged in by the participants. Something that is simultaneously part-Oriental, part-Polynesian, part-Occidental, yet also uniquely and completely "local," this sustained discussion process has created a sheltered port in the wider storms that attend environmental decision making. But there is something else as well. Beyond the logic of solving problems lies something more ineffable and a part of the way we do things in Hawai'i. Consensus builds trusting communities and heals and strengthens places. In this way, the body politic's sense of hope is renewed.

19

Beat the Dog!

Sometime in the very near future, after I have discovered a few more explorations, adventures, diversions, and entertainments with the likes of Louie Chang, Russell Kokubun, and Kem Lowry and properly field-tested another dozen good justifications and rationalizations, I intend to pen the definitive book on the art and science of chore avoidance. My tentative title is *Shirking Work: 101 Artful Ways to Avoid Rat Race in Paradise*. I suspect the book will be an instant best-seller in the Islands and, according to my wife Carolyn, I'm the perfect guy to write it.

Take the latest addition to my growing list of excuses. For the past few weeks my neighbor, Mr. Nato Furukake, has been asking me to trim the branches of our overhanging avocado tree, which, no matter how much I prune it, has a certain predilection for growing straight through his back window. A minor irritation, to my way of thinking, but for him an annual complaint and for the two of us, a seasonal negotiation.

Most years, I eventually get around to lopping off some of the more unruly foliage. It's a painful act but it has to be done or else the Furukake house will be swallowed up by the rain forest that is waiting to sprout any time civilized people let their guard down. But not this year. Or at least not quite yet. No negotiating and no tree pruning. In fact, no roof caulking, garage sweeping, weed whacking, window washing, car waxing, or oil changing. Basically (and here comes my most creative excuse to date), I've been in training.

For years, I had been thinking about joining that strange, howling, and slightly demented pack of water rats that annually jumps in the ocean at San Souci Beach near the old Kaimana Hotel and then emerges like waterlogged apparitions nearly two and a half miles later at Duke Kahanamoku Beach in front of the Hilton Hawaiian Village. The "Annual Waikīkī Rough Water Swim" is to local swimmers what the Boston Marathon is to the nation's runners: a clarion call to test one's personal best against both the elements and a bunch of aquatic lunatics.

The idea is this. You start out early in the morning when you are still half-asleep, hurl your body into the surf, swim 750 yards out through the Kapua Channel to a large channel buoy, turn right, swim 1.4 miles on the outside of the reef that runs the length of Waikīkī, and then turn right again and cover the remaining 925 yards to the Hilton. If it is a good year, you will miss the fierce currents, large waves, strong tides, and flotillas of stinging jellyfish that the race organizers warn about in their flyer. Unspoken, of course, is the nagging fear of large predatory sea creatures that might view a thousand thrashing humans as something akin to appetizers nicely arrayed at a buffet table. In the immortal words of Ken Dodd, "Honolulu has everything: sand for the children, sun for the wife, and sharks for the wife's mother."

Knowing all this, I filled out the registration, signed the liability waiver, paid my twenty bucks, and started training.

Down at the Nuʻuanu YMCA, which I affectionately think of as my "club," I met other aspiring rough-water racers. Like me, some of them were staving off the inevitable forces of gravity and entropy through a daily regimen of swimming. By any stretch of the imagination, we were an odd group. A retired policeman and a professor of tropical agriculture. An accountant with the local United Way and an electrical contractor. An overweight pediatrician and the owner of a laundromat. Each day before dawn, we would chuck ourselves into the Y's pool and crank out an hour or more of laps. After swimming, we would adjourn to Tanaka's Taste Buds, the Y's little food concession, to have a light breakfast and talk tactics.

Harry, the contractor, had done the Rough Water Swim twice before and immediately assumed a coachlike status with the rest of us. He assured us that 80 percent of all the swimmers who start the race finish it, and that most of those who don't are eventually found. "But you guys?" he promised, "you won't have no problems if you take her nice and steady and don't try to burn the course." Then he paused and said parenthetically, "And provided you stay away from the weird things out there 'cause they slow you down."

Six cups of coffee froze midway between table and lips. Six sets of eyes peered at Harry. Harry sipped his tea. "Weird things?" whispered Hiroko, the accountant. Then Harry told us about "Cow Man," a guy who does the swim each year with a set of buffalo horns on his head and who likes to stop swimmers out in the middle of the ocean to chat. Not to be outdone, another aquanaut sometimes transforms himself into "Pig Man" and wears a fake snout and a rubber cap with a squiggly tail sewn on the back. Then there was the dog.

Each year, explained Harry, some guy in that squirming mob of swimmers sneaks his Irish setter into the race. No one knows who he is or where the setter comes from. No one sees him do it. But in a testimonial to enduring relationships, man and mutt both complete the 2.38-mile race. Even as Harry brought all this up, a light bulb suddenly clicked on deep inside my cranium. The perfect goal for the race: beat the dog.

Over the next few months, I threw myself into more physical and mental conditioning. I swam at the Y weekdays and on weekends hit the ocean. I ran track, pushed weights, changed my diet to tofu and vegetables, and then changed it back again when someone told me I should eat a lot of meat. Most of all, I looked for dogs. Canines in general, and Irish setters in particular, were the enemy. Encountering one, I would put on my fiercest game face, give the animal a steely, withering stare, and count on it to pass the word along to whatever pooch was gearing up to swim against me.

On race day, I drove down to San Souci Beach two hours early to scope out water conditions and fine-tune my strategy. The ocean was flat, but a couple of race organizers told me to expect strong currents and big swells. The swimmers, he said, would go out in staggered heats five minutes apart, with the fastest swimmers in Group A and the slowest in Group E. I was in Group E along with Hiroko, our paunchy pediatrician friend, and Laundromat Larry. I figured to take things slow to the first turn, pick up speed on the long outside stretch, and then sprint for the finish.

Twenty minutes before the race, I scanned the growing crowd. Each swimmer had a race number conspicuously printed in large letters on the back of his or her calf. A race official came by, wrote mine out with a waterproof marker pen, gave me a bright yellow swim cap, and urged me to wear it during the race. All of these preparations, I presumed, were to facilitate body retrieval.

With ten minutes to go, I again inspected the swelling number of swimmers and looked for my competition. I saw a cluster of athletes from the Waikīkī Swim Club smearing sunscreen on each other's backs. I spotted Cow Man deep in conversation with Pig Man, sharing their respective views of life in the barnyard, no doubt. I spotted a couple of lean ex-Olympians stretching and bending their way through warm-ups. Mostly, though, I scrutinized everyone's lower extremities looking for a set of four-of-a-kind legs with luxurious red hair.

Finally, it was race time. A small cannon was fired and Group A hit the water. A few minutes later, Group B went off and then, in short order, Groups C and D. At last it was our turn. I looked down the beach at the hundred or so Group E swimmers. Quite a few beer bellies, bow legs, and bald heads but no shaggy red hair. No friendly doggy face and no wagging tail. A bad sign. I might actually have to compete with the humans.

And then suddenly, after months of training, we were off. I thrashed through the first hundred yards, found my rhythm, and settled into a steady crawl. At the first buoy, I completed my turn and picked up the pace. Earnestly, I looked around at my fellow swimmers, peering at their leg numbers when one of them passed me or I passed them. After fifty minutes, I caught up with some of the stragglers from Groups D and C and even raced past a few of them. At one hour and twenty-five minutes, I hit the second large buoy and turned right.

And then, in the surge and chop of the final thousand yards, in the small slit of clear space just above the water sloshing around in my leaky goggles, I caught a glimpse of something red. I turned up my kick, put some extra draw into my stroke, and powered myself closer. Sure enough. Four legs steadily paddling away. A regal nose held high out of the water.

The dog.

Deep into the final reserves of strength that Coach Harry said we would need to finish the race, I cranked it up one last notch. One hundred yards from the finish, I was side by side with Fido. I glanced at him and he looked at me and then he seemed to turn on the canine equivalent of an afterburner. Paws against arms and feet, we made for the finish line in a dead heat.

Even as I pulled up on the beach, exhausted, cramped, and dehydrated, I heard the applause. I ran the last few yards to the finish chute to record my official time and saw dozens of people yelling and cheering. Not for me, of course, but for my Irish friend who trotted through the chute as if he had just won the Publisher's Clearinghouse. Dumbfounded, I watched as he shook himself off, sat down for a scratch, rolled in the sand, stood up, and flopped his way through several admiring fans to join his waiting master, our old pal Harry.

The race is behind me now and I'm powerfully pleased to be finished with it. Maybe I'll do it next year just to get even with Harry and his water-brained dog. Meanwhile I keep postponing that day of reckoning when, pruning saw in hand, I will have to finally trim those strong-willed avocado branches away from Mr. Furukake's back window. When he does call, though, I'll tell him that I have to wait just a few more days because I'm deep in the midst of serious postswim recovery.

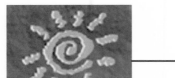

20

Hot Times

Every once in a while when the prevailing northeast trade winds absent themselves, Honolulu experiences what locals call "Kona weather." Kona weather is hot, humid, and windless. It makes people listless (and a bit grouchier than usual) and it can last an hour, a day, or a month. To avoid complete lethargy during Kona weather, most Honolulu people stay inside near their air conditioners and ice makers. It is that time of year when local people put in an extra eight hours of effort and show America why Hawai'i really is the home of the four-day work week.

But not everyone.

Amidst a torpid heat that is draped over the city like a baggy sweatshirt, four of us are wandering around downtown at midday. It is really not a good time to be out, but our mission is essential. For the third year in a row, my buddy Keith and I are taking a personal history walk through old Honolulu. If things stay true to previous years, this tour will end up with a monstrous, immobilizing lunch at a Chinese restaurant and give all four of us the perfect excuse we need to avoid going back to work.

Our guides in this endeavor are two of Hawai'i's most interesting and accomplished people. Clinton "Tink" Ashford and C. F. "Frank" Damon, ages 71 and 70, respectively, are both lawyers. Not only are they lawyers, they are senior partners in two of Hawai'i's best-known law firms. Ashford & Wriston is located in a building just across from the State Capitol. The Damon Key Bocken Leong Kupchak firm is a block away overlooking O'ahu's commercial and financial district. Despite the fact that their law firms occasionally go head-to-head in court, the two are good friends.

Part of their friendship is based on a deep and shared connection to places the rest of us vaguely and dismissively lump together as "downtown." Urban Honolulu tends to get disregarded by travel writers, tourists, and even by many locals. Some of this is completely understandable. Encompassed by a near-perfect year-round climate (Kona weather being the rude exception), embraced by a sparkling ocean, soothed by cool, verdant mountains, who really cares about a bunch of old streets and buildings anyway? Actually, Damon and Ashford do. And, after three years of exploring some of Honolulu's peculiar nooks and crannies, so do Keith and I.

Frank, tall and lean as a sapling, is a descendant of Samuel C. Damon, a famous missionary who arrived in Hawai'i in 1842 and became an early champion of racial tolerance at a time when most Westerners viewed Hawaiians, Chinese, and Japanese as backward and primitive peoples. Samuel Damon thought different, said so, and got in trouble because of it. His other special passion was the plight of seafarers. He ministered to the men of the whaling fleet, built and maintained churches, befriended the disadvantaged, founded a home for elderly and disabled sailors, and created *The Friend,* an early and influential newspaper read throughout the Pacific.

Similarly, Tink Ashford, with his full mane of snow-white hair, can trace his lineage to the Wilder family, founders of the Inter-Island Steamship Company, and to Clarence Wilder Ashford, who became an important figure in the political dramas surrounding the final days of the Kingdom of Hawai'i. Ashford, along with other Royalists, opposed the overthrow of the monarchy, was exiled in 1895 by the Republic of Hawai'i, and then returned to the Islands several years after annexation to become a respected judge in the newly created Territory of Hawai'i.

At the moment, much of this personal, social, and historical past is coming into immediate focus as we poke around downtown in the noontime heat. Specifically, we are at the corner of Merchant and Nu'uanu Streets near two local watering holes called Murphy's Bar and Grill and O'Toole's Pub. Both of these Celtic establishments are located in a part of Honolulu that is rich with history—if you know where to look for it.

Which our guides do. Tink, Frank, Keith, and I are on our knees examining the sidewalk in front of Murphy's. The curbstones, Tink points out, are made of local "blue rock" that was quarried by convicts in territorial days. In turn, the white sidewalk is made of old ballast blocks that were brought to Honolulu in schooners plying the China trade and carrying, in addition to silk, sandalwood, and plantation workers, opium smuggled in some of the stones that were hollowed out for just that purpose. Also embedded in the rocks are two worn-out steel pins, the remains of old hitching rings from the days when everyone who was anyone in Hawai'i rode a horse.

Honolulu of horse and buggy days was a notoriously bawdy, scandal-ridden, and, in the vernacular of the time, "dissolute" place. Walking these very same streets a century or more ago, we would have found a thriving commerce in spices and commodities and a dozen dance houses, grogshops, and saloons with names like The Devil's Den and the White Swan occupying what is today the habitat of bankers and architects. Standing here in the era of first and second generations of Ashfords and Damons, in fact, we might have seen the Blond Hotel (the first of many brothels, now occupied by another law firm) and even witnessed on this precise street the love triangle and murder that led to Hawai'i's first jury trial.

Even with its own active temperance society, Honolulu appears to have been a drinking man's paradise. At a place called Cunha's Alley just a block away from where we are now inspecting sidewalk stones, we would have found another set of taverns, one of which was the Union Saloon run by Mr. Cunha himself, inventor of the drink now called the old-fashioned. Next to the Union, in 1832, King Kamehameha III and some of his cohorts would eventually throw the biggest, wildest party in the history of Honolulu by going on a three-day bender and drinking thirty-two barrels of whiskey. And down the street in the other direction, at the corner of Hotel and Nu'uanu, we would have found the only place in Hawai'i—and maybe the only place anywhere—with a saloon on all four corners of a major intersection.

Today, Honolulu is a far more sedate place with its own endearing ways of doing things. In fact, Honolulu is still probably best thought of as a slightly overgrown cow town with a few urban pretensions that are entirely excusable given its strategic mid-Pacific location and its unique cross-cultural history. But Honolulu is also a place that has kept itself to a manageable scale and retained its sense of human intimacy. That tradition continues in odd and occasionally embarrassing ways.

Even as we are poking around in the heat looking at old curbstones and tethering rings, an acquaintance of mine walks up. He is a *kanaka maoli* man who I happen to know is descended from royalty and who now runs a computer company. He is with another person I have met on one or two occasions, a Singaporean who came to Hawai'i several years ago and who owns a very successful Vietnamese restaurant.

As we exchange pleasantries and I start to sputter out an explanation about why we are crawling around on the sidewalk not far from Murphy's Bar and Grill, two friends of Tink's come by, see us, and stop to say hello. Small world. Fred and Erminie Gartley are in town from Maui to do some business. As it turns out, one of Fred's immediate ancestors, Peter C. "Pop Corn" Jones, was a prominent Honolulu businessman and a member of the Provisional Government, the very same group that chased Ashford's grandfather out of the Islands in 1895. About the time we get to the part about opium-filled ballast stones, two of Keith's friends who are headed for lunch at O'Toole's walk up and politely inquire about what's going on.

Eventually, the little knot of people that has collected around us breaks up and we continue our circuit around old Honolulu. We visit the site of Samuel Damon's original home at a place called Chaplain Lane, then wander back to where Tink Ashford's father, Huron Kanoelani Ashford, had his law office when he served in the Territorial Legislature. Then we meander past the Stangenwald Building (home to Hawai'i's first elevator, which achieved the astounding speed of 25 feet per minute), the old fort off Fort Street Mall where King David Kalākaua's grandfather was hanged for poisoning his wife, and to the statue of Robert Wilcox, who led the Royalists in their resistance to annexation.

An hour later, wilted and hungry, we finally wander into the Ken Fong Hong Kong Style Noodle House and order two pitchers of ice water, some lemon chicken, beef with oyster sauce, ong choy with bean curd, squid with sour cabbage, rice, and tea. As we settle down to our lunch, Frank pulls out a flask of seventy-year-old 'ōkolehao, finely aged, home-brewed, Hawaiian-style whiskey. In the old days, 'ōkolehao was home-brewed using the same recipes that Kentucky moonshiners used. A cask of this special-occasion stuff has been handed down through several generations of Damons. He pours a little in each of our teacups and proposes a toast. "To good friends," says Frank as he raises his cup. "To temperance and demon rum," says Keith as he clinks cups with the rest of us. "And to hot times in the old town," says Tink, just as a steaming plate of lemon chicken arrives.

21

Bull's-Eye

I am walking along the water's edge early in the morning. The place is a small stretch of beach at a spot called Onekahakaha just outside of Hilo on the island of Hawai'i. As the sun comes up, sandpipers skitter across the sand and hunt for crabs. Small waves lap against the shore. Like so many other places in Hawai'i, the beach is quiet and remote, the moment peaceful and dreamlike.

It could all change in a flash, of course. Immersed as we are in Hawai'i's manifold beauties, it is easy to forget the dangers that come with our unique island geography. The reminders usually come when we least expect them. Tectonic pressures build up under the archipelago, the ground shivers, buildings tremble, and sidewalks fold like an accordion. A volcanic fissure opens up in the district of Puna and acres of productive papaya farms are burned to the ground. Prevailing wind and water currents shift and ever so suddenly a hurricane tracks into the island of Kaua'i.

At 2:00 A.M. on April 1, 1946, nature flexed a different sort of muscle. It started with an earthquake that rumbled across the Aleutian Trench off the coast of Alaska, setting in motion a lethal chain of events. A tidal wave 115 feet high carried away a Coast Guard crew and their concrete lighthouse on Unimak Island sixty miles from the quake's epicenter. Five hours and 2,300 miles later, just as the people of Hawai'i were starting their day, waves generated from that same quake smashed into the Islands.

Daniel Walker, a retired professor of geophysics from the University of Hawai'i, has spent most of his professional life studying the 1946 and other local tsunamis. From his home high atop Pūpūkea Ridge on O'ahu's North Shore, he reads technical journals and historical documents, watches the ocean, and helps the local civil defense agency with their emergency preparedness plans. On average, he says, we can expect two or three potentially destructive tsunamis someplace in the Pacific each year. Then a worried look crosses his face. "It's been thirty years and most people in Hawai'i have forgotten what a real tsunami is all about."

But Walker hasn't. A trim, energetic man, he directs the Tsunami Memorial Institute, a one-man organization that provides educational materials to teachers, students, and community groups. He points to a laminated tsunami map he published. The map shows the Hawaiian Islands dead center in the Pacific basin surrounded by the volcanic "ring of fire" and inward radiating concentric circles. On his map, Hawai'i is five hours from Alaska, seven hours from Kamchatka, and fifteen hours from South America. "In tsunami terms," he says, "we are a bull's-eye."

When Walker and other scientists describe tsunamis, they tend to use technical terms to explain them. Tsunamis are "seismic sea waves." Mechanically, they are always caused by the same thing: a sudden rise or fall in the earth's crust and a consequent displacement of the water column above.

Earthquakes and undersea landslides are the usual culprits, though large asteroids and meteors falling to earth à la the film *Deep Impact* would certainly do the trick.

Once it gets started, a tsunami wave radiates out from the source of the disturbance at speeds that can approach 500 mph. The word "wave" is a bit of a misnomer here. A tsunami is more like a massive flood. As the sudden "gush" of water approaches land, the wave gains traction and begins to slow down. Height increases. The mass of water then washes in and out with tremendous power. A tsunami's impacts on land are measured in two ways. "Innundation" is the horizontal distance inland that is deluged. "Runup" is the measure of a wave's height or amplitude.

Between Unimak Island and the Hawaiian chain, the 1946 Aleutian wave shed some of its power but little of its mass. It reached a runup of fifty-four feet on an uninhabited section of Moloka'i. Elsewhere, the wave caught people on the shoreline unaware or washed up in coastal population centers. Six people were killed on O'ahu. Another thirty-one died on Maui and Kaua'i. In all, 160 people lost their lives. Hardest hit was the little city of Hilo on the island of Hawai'i. Photos of the wave taken during and after recorded the devastation for posterity.

One of them, touched up, colorized, and magnified, is particularly haunting. The photographer, a barber named Cecilo Licos, just happened to be standing on Ponahawai Street with a camera facing the waterfront a few hundred feet away when the third wave of the tsunami hit. In the photo, twenty people are running toward him, their faces etched with terror. Some of them are looking over their shoulders. Behind them, a thirty-foot wall of water is crashing into downtown Hilo. The wave is higher than the coconut trees fronting Hilo Bay.

Twenty-five miles north of Hilo, the same set of waves devastated the small plantation town of Laupāhoehoe. Set on a low, open peninsula of land just a few feet above sea level, Laupāhoehoe was particularly defenseless. That morning, students and teachers gathered at the local school built on the small tongue of land by the sea, as they did every day. While they assembled, surf crashed against a seawall. No one was unduly alarmed. Then, suddenly, the water rose in a massive, powerful surge that ripped buildings off foundations and carried five teachers and sixteen students away. One of those teachers was Fred Cruz, a classmate of my father-in-law.

Back in Hilo, the tsunami wreaked even more havoc. Boulders the size of automobiles were tossed into the air like confetti. Houses were demolished. Whole buildings were swept out to sea. Some waves boiled over the tops of buildings. Others bent railroad tracks as if they were noodles. On the edge of the Wailoa River, which runs through downtown Hilo, people ran for high ground even as the river filled with bodies and rubble. One woman was washed out of her bathtub and left standing in the street stark naked. Dozens of others were sucked out to sea. Some floated on makeshift rafts of debris and were rescued. Most drowned.

Fifty years later, recollections of that disaster still linger. Hilo is a small town and memories run deep. People talk about 1946 as if it was yesterday. The sagas of those who died and those who survived are now commemorated at the recently opened Pacific Tsunami Museum. Located in a former and very stately bank building, the museum houses memorabilia from the '46 catastrophe, virtual reality simulations, and exhibits on the history, myths, legends, and science of tsunamis. The museum's official poster bears the remarkable photo taken by Cecilo Licos on Ponahawai Street.

More vivid still for the people of Hilo is the tsunami of May 23, 1960. That wave, generated by an 8.5 earthquake in Chile, washed across the Pacific and slammed into three continents. Once more, perhaps because of the unique bathymetry of its bay, the devastation in Hilo was acute. As the wave rolled in and out, it took the form of a tidal bore with a vertical wall at its head. A massive front of seawater flooded into downtown Hilo for a second time. The local power plant exploded. Banks of parking meters were bent flat. Whole city blocks were swept clean of their structures and sixty-one more people died.

Today, Hawai'i is probably overdue for another catastrophic tsunami. "Because they are episodic and because we have occasional false alarms, people in Hawai'i get blasé about tidal waves," says Chip McCreery, a veteran tsunami tracker. "We even have a few kamikaze surfers who think you can ride them—which you can't." Like Dan Walker, McCreery has focused his life's work on the subject. And as geophysicist-in-charge at the Pacific Tsunami Warning Center in 'Ewa Beach on O'ahu, it is his job to examine incoming data and trigger the advisories, cautionaries, and warnings that Civil Defense relies on to prevent disasters.

McCreery, an affable and engaging man, spends most of his days inside a room full of maps and computers. At night, he is electronically tethered to beepers and cell phones. At the Center, he and his colleagues work their way through the real-time streams of seismic and water level data coming in from collection points all over the world. When an earthquake occurs, either locally or elsewhere, the Pacific Tsunami Warning Center goes on instant alert. "We work hard to achieve accuracy," he says, "but in fact, the most important thing we actually do is cancel events."

Nonetheless, false alarms are inevitable. On the morning of October 4, 1994, for example, all of us in Hawai'i woke up and, over breakfast, learned about an 8.2 quake off northern Japan. It took seven minutes for the seismic wave to travel to Hawai'i and, although most people would not have noticed it, says McCreery, the Islands actually moved up and down by a centimeter. When the earthquake went off in the middle of the night, McCreery was the first person through the Center's front door.

Twenty minutes later, as readings from Japan and Wake Island came in, they knew they had a big one. A Pacific-wide warning went up: a potentially destructive tsunami was predicted for 10:00 A.M. Hawai'i time. Island by island, civil defense authorities made their preparations and then turned the sirens on just as people were waking up. Newscasters excitedly told everyone to stay calm. Low-lying areas were evacuated and police rerouted traffic inland. Even so, says Dan Walker, there were at least 200 surfers in the water. Then people waited. The tsunami never came. Water lapped on the shore a few extra inches and then life returned to normal.

If history bears witness, it may not be like that the next time. Walking along the beach at Onekahakaha and warmed by the rising sun, one would never guess a tsunami is coming. But people with experience say you never turn your back on the sea. The ancient Hawaiian people had wisdom on this matter: " 'Ilili ke kai i ka 'ope'ope la, lilo; i lilo no he hāwāwā," meaning "The sea snatches the bundle. It is gone. It goes when one is not watchful."

So it will be when the next tsunami or hurricane or earthquake or lava flow changes the normally staid boundaries of our universe in the Hawaiian Islands.

22

Lava

Lava filled the ancient temple of Waha'ula yesterday destroying what many consider the most significant archaeological feature in Hawai'i Volcanoes National Park.

—*Honolulu Advertiser,* August 12, 1997

When friends from elsewhere contemplate a visit to Hawai'i, they invariably ask me to recommend one special thing they should see and do. My advice is always the same: get thee straight away to the volcanoes! And if time and stamina permit, do it on foot and with a backpack. Unless you come from Vesuvius in Italy or Mount St. Helens in the Northwest, Hawai'i's volcanoes will challenge and awe you. Even after spending most of my life in the Islands, the magic of these powerful geological engines still compels me. I go there often.

Part of it is the sheer mystery of tectonic plates, midocean hot spots, and the unimaginable time spans involved in Hawaiian island formation. Then there is the sacred side. The

145

volcanoes are a revered part of Hawai'i's cultural traditions embodied most concretely in the goddess Pele around whom myths and legends still swirl. Finally, there is the solitude. In the clutter of busy lives, an expedition to Hawai'i Volcanoes National Park is a journey through inner no less than outer geographies.

In 1980, for example, I slipped out of Honolulu for a week and hiked forty miles of the national park's coast. My route, mapped out well in advance, took me from the rain forests surrounding Kīlauea Caldera to the dry, surf-pounded shores of the Puna and Ka'ū Districts. I went to that rugged coast with two overriding intentions: to get away from meetings and phone calls and to see, firsthand, a hidden part of Hawai'i that I had only heard about from hunters and fishermen. I wasn't disappointed on either count.

Hawai'i Volcanoes National Park is a place of extraordinary contrasts. Vast stretches of old and new lava have created a terrain that, in some places, is lunar in its textures, colors, and composition. Elsewhere, trees and plants have taken root and formed a thick, green carpet of forest hiding birds, insects, and plants found no place else in the world. Everywhere the land is governed and ultimately dwarfed by Hawai'i's two active volcanoes, Mauna Loa and Kīlauea.

My journey in 1980 started, courtesy of a friend with a truck, at Hilina Pali, a cliff about 2,500 feet above sea level in the park's high chaparral area. There, amidst blossoming *'ohia* trees and the alarmed honkings of a pair of Hawaiian geese, I set off across the twisted flows of lava that make up the Ka'ū Desert. My goal was Kalapana, where my friend would meet me five days hence.

I headed west to a trail junction near a small cabin called Pepeiao and, from there, shuffled my way down to the coast through broomsedge and pili grass. At the place known as Nāpu'uonā'elemākule ("The Hills of the Old Men"), I turned east and spent the night at a seldom-visited place called Kālu'e. Blissfully alone, I remember swimming in the reef-fringed lagoon and eating a simple dinner in the lee of a tree. Later, in the sunset along the beach, I found two moray eels hanging on upright sticks surrounded by arrangements of shells and animal bones and then spent a disconcerting night hearing soft voices in a language I couldn't recognize.

Or was it the wind?

The District of Puna has multiple personalities, some moody, some coy, some fiery and tempestuous, some subdued and peaceful. All of them are dominated by Kīlauea Volcano's east rift, a long sear in the skin of the earth where viscous lavas periodically erupt and burn their way down to the sea. The rift is a deep and continuous fissure of superheated rock that extends some fifty miles downslope from the main caldera. Crossing the length of Puna, it is where most of Kīlauea's dramatic flank eruptions occur.

Hiking the edge of that rift, I found myself confronting those different personae in unexpected ways. Eager to get away from the peculiar shadows plaguing Kālu'e, I left at first light. I followed an ancient, unmarked path skirting sea cliffs and rock beaches and then rejoined the National Park Trail at the foot of Pu'ukapukapu, a mountain sacred to the followers of the god Lono. Slowly, I made my way to my next stop, Halapē.

On the Big Island, the molten power shooting up from the Earth's core permeates everything. Because the land is growing and changing, life is fresh and elemental. Wind, wave, rain, and sun grind away at the edges, but the fire that fuels the island's growth continues unabated. That slow accretion is magnificent to see, but it is also dangerous.

Halapē was, and still is, a place of breathtaking beauty. Situated at the eastern foot of Pu'ukapukapu, it commands stunning up-slope vistas of the Ka'ū Desert and the cliffs of Kīlauea.

In the other direction, the view opens out on the indigo waters of a seemingly protected seacoast. But looks are deceiving. On November 29, 1975—and not for the first time—the ground trembled, boulders the size of houses were tossed around like marbles, and an entire grove of coconut trees sank into the ocean. Campers died in the ensuing tsunami. The epicenter of that 7.2 earthquake was Kalapana, my destination.

From Halapē, I set off on the long, hot, waterless part of the trek that hugs the Puna coast. Truthfully speaking, many of my recollections have blurred. I am at a loss to recall the food I ate, the other travelers I may have met, or the swarms of gnats and flies that surely plagued me. Although I can bring back the feel of the heat of the day and the sight of stars filling the sky at rocky outcrops near ʻĀpua Point and Kealakomo, most of the particulars have faded.

But not all.

These many years later, I still know, sharp as a crack of thunder, the smell, feel, and touch of the intricately tangled lavas I passed on that very youngest of Hawaiian geographies. I remember large flows of *pāhoehoe,* their billowy folds convoluted into the edges of other flows or braided into pieces of rope the size of a building. I recall the glaciers of hot rock that had spilled over Kīlauea's sides leaving mounds of jagged *ʻaʻā* at the bottom. And I can still visualize one particular hill of clinkers proportioned like a railroad train and, next to it, a long basin that looked as if they had been excavated by controlled blasts of dynamite.

The fierce and barren beauties of these lavas come back to me now. So too do the sparkle of feldspar, the wink of olivine, and the gunmetal glint of newly made rock. To walk on those scarred, pockmarked stretches of lava is to wander amidst igneous beginnings and endings. It was, and remains for all who go there, a personal journey through the primal dreams of our species.

Locals and visitors alike report this regularly. Stones thrown up from the earth and cooled in the fresh trades tug at the human imagination. Some see shapes: animals, faces, monsters, gods and goddesses. Others imagine the lava as blocks of steel or jagged, razor-edged weapons of war. And for some, the vents, cracks, fissures, fractures, cones, tubes, and ledges are just the skin of a much larger life that informs our own small species.

Whatever we visualize, we know that the contours of these natural wonders are transitory. In Hawai'i, the land as we see it is a temporary arrangement. It is "on loan" from nature. Sometimes the changes created are wondrous and stunning. Sometimes they are painful.

Part of my route in 1980 followed a marked but little used seaside trail, a path that in olden times was a major thoroughfare for Hawaiians traversing the districts on foot. There, amongst the harsh lavas of this least-visited part of Hawai'i, I encountered the ruins of house sites, fishing shrines, canoe launches, sheds, and dance platforms. I slept there with ancient voices whispering at me.

On the fourth day, not far from an inviting grove of shade trees, I came to the ancient *heiau* of Waha'ula, a place sacred and terrifying to the communities that once lived there. Set in the splendor of a vast lava field, Waha'ula was a *luakini* temple where human sacrifices were conducted. Built in the thirteenth century by Pā'ao, a conquering chief from Tahiti, it was later appropriated by Kamehameha the Great, who dedicated it to his war god Kūkā'ilimoku. Later still, it would become one of the last places where the old *kanaka maoli* gods were worshiped publically.

Walking around the temple, gazing at the waterworn boulders by the shore and seeing the rock remains of what may have been the oracle tower, I could feel the terror. Here, with strictly observed rituals, ordinary people from the lower classes were selected by an elite group of body catchers called the *Mū*. The victims were then killed by the priests who, through sacrifice and blood, cleansed the temple for other ceremonies.

On my long, hot journey down the Puna coast, however, Waha'ula became a place of rest and contemplation, a spot to sit and ponder times long gone. In the shade of a *hala* tree I could daydream of the civilization that flourished here for a thousand years. I could visualize the fishermen who hunted beyond the reef, the families who observed the intimacies of their community, and the farmers who carried soil from the uplands to cultivate crops in small lava depressions.

On the last day of my journey, I made off at dawn for Kalapana where I would meet my friend. I passed small settlements and the scattered homes of local people. I accepted a ride for a few miles from an old Chinese man driving a decrepit Chevrolet with no back window and then walked a bit farther when he stopped to visit friends.

In the late afternoon, parched and sunburned, I puffed into Kalapana and straight away made for the Walter Yamaguchi General Store, where I drank down a quart carton of orange juice. Then I left Kalapana with my friend and flew back to Honolulu, purged of my accumulated twentieth-century demons and deeply refreshed.

Today, most of the coastal trail I walked in 1980 is gone. Beginning in 1983, the rift poured out billions of cubic yards of fresh lava, burying homes, churches, and cars. Most of the old homesteads were abandoned and overrun in November 1986. More homes were picked off by the lava flows of '87, '88, and '89. Most of Kalapana Village, including Walter Yamaguchi's store, went down in 1990.

On August 12, 1997, just before dawn, a fresh stream of advancing lava coursed through the rectangular structures of Waha'ula Heiau, filled the enclosure with molten stone, poured over the seaward wall, and then joined another black and orange tributary flowing into the ocean. The *heiau* that had lasted 700 years was swallowed, even as a new peninsula of land was formed on the expanding shores of the island of Hawai'i.

Heartbeats

Discovery and insight come in strange ways and at odd times. In Hawai'i, it could happen like this. One evening after dinner you decide to take a walk around Diamond Head, one of Honolulu's most famous landmarks. The route you follow swings around the backside of Diamond Head along Monsarrat Avenue and past the old military reservation called Fort Ruger. Ruger, named after an 1870s superintendent of West Point, has a venerable military history but feels more like a park. As on most other evenings, there are other joggers and walkers out enjoying what is, for all practical purposes, an ordinary evening in Hawai'i.

In the twilight, the crimson sky dissolves into a hundred pinks and purples. Birds flit through the trees on their way home for the night. The air is thick with the scents of plumeria and mock orange. As you come closer to the old fort itself, however, you begin to hear an odd and disconcerting booming that could be a peal of distant thunder. Then, just as you come upon the Fort Ruger Chapel, a great rumble billows out of the tiny wooden structure and rolls across the sidewalk exactly where you are walking.

After a brief moment of recovery, you wander over to the chapel to investigate the source of all this sound and when you poke your head inside the chapel, you see drums. Fifteen of them. Fifteen larger and smaller drums with fifteen larger and smaller drummers of different ages, genders, and races pounding away in a complex earthy cadence that immediately works its way into the very marrow of your being.

Normally, drums are things to be quietly admired from a discrete distance or ignored altogether. In the hands of the 8-year-old neighbor kid, they are a major irritant. In the right setting, they rise up and make for great jazz and rock and roll. But this particular drumming is different. It is vibrant and primeval, filled with power, suffused with energy. It is impossible to walk away. You stay and watch and a new part of your education as a world citizen begins.

What you will be seeing, hearing, and absorbing through the vibrating floorboards of the old Fort Ruger Chapel is Kenny and Chizuko Endo's intermediate-level *taiko* class hard at it as they conduct their Thursday night practice. *Taiko* is the generic name for both the Japanese drum and for the highly focused and infinitely subtle art of Japanese drumming. This class, however, is anything but professional. It is a potpourri of Island faces made up of a schoolteacher, a lawyer and his wife, a couple of gardeners, and half a dozen other men, women, boys, and girls. Four of these drum zealots are Adler women.

Carolyn and our three teenage daughters, Corey, Dana, and Kelly, have been taking *taiko* lessons for several years. For our kids, who are half-Japanese, *taiko* is a logical extension of their Japanese language training, and of aikido, the art of self-defense that they have studied for many years at a dojo in our neighborhood. Aikido and *taiko* share a common warrior ancestry. Like Scottish bagpipes, *taiko* drums were first used to terrify enemies on the battlefield. Later, Japanese farming communities defined their territory by the distance that a *taiko* could be heard. Later still, *taiko* were incorporated into both everyday community celebrations and those special rituals that used the drum's deep reverberations to represent the voice of the Buddha.

Today in Japan, and in places as disparate as Burlington, Vermont, and Adelaide, South Australia, *taiko* is both a revived cultural practice and a creative new performing art. And thanks in great part to people like the Endos, Hawai'i has become something of a *taiko* "Mecca." Several drumming schools are in operation, and on most weekends you will usually find a performance or practice session going on someplace in the Islands.

On this particular Thursday night, Chizuko Endo is leading the class. She claps a tiny hand cymbal she is holding to get the class' attention. Feet planted squarely, knees slightly bent in a style familiar to students of the martial arts, the drummers assume their ready position, hold their sticks out, and wait. Then Chizuko gives the signal and the practice pattern begins. Fifteen sets of sticks descend in unison and hit the skin of their drums close to dead center. Slowly, the group warms to the task and moves through the core rhythms that form the backbone of *taiko.*

For the next hour the class will take on progressively more difficult practice pieces. Some of Chizuko's sets call for complex choreography in which students switch drums without breaking stride. They and their classmates will slowly move around the semicircle of instruments and criss-cross through the larger drums positioned in the center of the circle. Sometimes Kenny or Chizuko will have students leap and twirl on their way to the next drum or give each student a little bit of time for a "drum solo" while the others keep a background beat.

In the mixing and swirling of tones and beats, each drummer manages to find his or her unique voice with the drum at hand. The Nagado-daiko is the standard performing and festival drum made with skins that are tacked down on what looks like a large pickle barrel. The smaller Odeko-daiko are made with staves. The Hira-daiko are orchestral instruments. They resemble common rock and roll snare drums but have a much richer sound. The mother-of-all drums is the Odaiko, which weighs several hundred pounds and is played on a horizontal stand, sometimes by two people, one on each side. With its deep, complex reverberations, it holds an especially honored place when a *taiko* group performs.

Using these basic instruments, Kenny and Chizuko Endo, founders of The Taiko Center of the Pacific, are constantly blending the old and the new. They are especially adept at getting their students to absorb traditional understandings even as they encourage modern experimentation. Most of the Endo's innovations are musical, but *taiko* innovations come in other forms as well. One of those is now sprawling across our living room floor in the form of *"gomikan-taiko."*

Loosely translated, *gomikan* means "trash can." Using various-sized garbage tubs, rolls of packing tape, old broom handles, and an assortment of exacto knives, rasps, and chisels, the Endos have taught their students how to make inexpensive, homemade practice drums. One result is the "Honolulu Adler Taiko Quartet," which performs nightly with backup from the neighbor's three dogs.

At this particular Thursday practice, I watch Corey, our oldest, who is leaving soon to spend a year at the University of Surrey in England. The physics and harmonics of *taiko* drumming present all manner of challenges, but it is also, at its most elemental, just plain fun. Hands fly through the air. Brown hair arcs behind her as she shifts her weight. Arms swinging, she bangs the drum with focused energy and dances through her sets, a broad smile on her lovely face.

Several nights later, Carolyn and I and the kids walk down the street to the local Koganjii Buddhist Temple, which is holding a neighborhood O-Bon celebration here in Mānoa Valley. The dance is well in progress when we get there. Several hundred men and women (including two grandmas chasing down a runaway two-year-old) are sitting on benches or milling around the periphery munching on ears of roasted corn, buckwheat noodles in little cardboard trays, and sizzling barbecued beef on sticks. Meanwhile, dozens of dancers in brightly colored kimonos are steadily circling around the decorated *yagura* tower in the center of the courtyard. Hundreds of lanterns and folded paper blossoms have been strung overhead.

In Hawai'i, O-Bon is another of the many regular cultural junctures where East and West converge. Local people steadfastly celebrate their own heritages, but also grow up participating in the customs and celebrations of other groups. That is why, in addition to learning their own traditions, Portuguese and Filipinos take up Hawaiian canoe paddling, Koreans and Hawaiians learn Chinese lion dances, and everyone goes to the neighborhood O-Bon dance.

At an O-Bon celebration all people, regardless of age or ethnicity, are encouraged to participate. O-Bon is both a happy and reverential time. According to Japanese Buddhist traditions, its purpose is to guide the souls of departed family members back home and properly commemorate and remember them. The dance is only one part of the festival. During O-Bon, graves are visited, relatives are invited over, and lanterns with lit candles are floated down rivers and streams.

But our main purpose tonight is to enjoy our little community's dance and to hear some former students of Kenny Endo who have been invited to perform during an intermission in the dance. We listen and watch as a newly formed *taiko* troupe performs both traditional and interpretive numbers. At the end of their performance, there is thunderous applause for the drummers, the drums, and the magic that infuses itself into the old rhythms come to life.

Late in the evening we walk back home, tired, quiet, and lost in our own private contemplations. For myself, it is Corey I am pondering. Discovery comes in strange ways and at odd times. She leaves for England soon and is already starting to pack. With her will go an oddly shaped, hand-sewn cloth pouch that will inevitably draw scrutiny at Customs. It contains her wooden aikido weapons and two sets of homemade *taiko* sticks.

I will carry this bag to the airport for her and make sure that it gets through security. Since she was a small girl, she has been told by her aikido teachers that the staff, sword, and dagger are extensions of her soul. So too with the *taiko* sticks, which carry the secret knowledge that connects drumbeats to the heartbeats of those who have come before.

The Back of Beyond

It's 6 A.M. as Aloha Island Air Flight 1428 taxis down the runway, lifts off, and turns east into the darkness. The flying time from O'ahu to the island of Lāna'i is just over twenty minutes. By the time we are aloft in the DASH-8, there is a crease of scarlet on the horizon. Halfway to Maui, a tawny light spills through the window.

One of the people in the plane, a skinny guy with a wispy mustache, asks if this is the champagne breakfast flight. Beneath the thrumming of the propellers, and despite the hour, there are chuckles and grins. The steward laughs and hands him a little cup of pineapple-orange punch that tastes like Kool-Aid and bears an uncanny resemblance to a melted popsicle.

Most of this morning's seats are occupied by local folks going to Lāna'i for the opening of the Axis deer hunting season. The others are construction workers, families with children returning home, and a couple of Australian visitors. The attire is camouflage, T-shirts, slippers, and shorts. The discussions are about ordinary things: the island's new high-school teacher; the latest editorial in the *Lāna'i Times;* and the best place for locals to eat out on Lāna'i, there being exactly three. One of the Lāna'ians and a hunter are having an animated discussion on the best way to catch and cook mullet. "Steamed with black bean sauce," says one. "Ah, just sprinkle 'em wid shoyu, onions, and salt and bake 'em," says the other.

Soon, the plane banks and descends. Alenka Remec and I clamber down the steps and are met by Brian Valley in his pickup truck. Alenka and Brian work for The Nature Conservancy, which has a small office on the island. Our ostensible objective is to visit a patch of rare forest at a place called Kānepu'u and meet its caretakers, a group called Hui Mālama Pono O Lāna'i. The real adventure, however, is poking around on an out-of-the-way island where all things present inextricably loop back to the past.

Even by Hawai'i standards, Lāna'i is obscure. I've heard people who should know better refer to it as "Dogpatch" or the "Back of Beyond." What they usually mean is that the island is off the beaten path and steeped in traditions that remain largely invisible to outsiders. Fact is that Lāna'i is what all of us in the 50th State once were and what, if you scratch away the surface sensibilities of the late 1990s, we still are: a small, rural, and intensely intimate community.

From the airport, we head up to Lāna'i City. Vast stretches of fallow, stubbly pineapple fields surround us. With a scant 140 square miles of land, and situated in the rain shadow of Maui, Lāna'i is one of the smallest and driest of Hawai'i's main islands. Most of Lāna'i's residents live at higher elevations where it is cooler and wetter. As it was fifty years ago, people still prefer the tidy little battened plantation homes with corrugated metal roofs that were popular back then. Lāna'i "City" is a bit of a euphemism and overstatement if you hail from a place like Philadelphia or St. Louis. The city is about fifteen blocks square.

In front of many of the homes you will also notice either an embalmed Jeep, or wooden rooster hutches, or both. I have it on good authority that Lāna'i is home to more fighting chickens and functioning WWII-era Willys than any other place in the world. Nearly all of the Jeeps are serviced at the island's one gas station. Chickens come and go into someone's frying pan, but the island's 2,800 people tend to stay. They are mostly first-, second-, and third-generation Filipinos and Japanese whose roots are in the old pineapple culture.

True to plantation traditions, everyone on Lāna'i knows everyone else. Not only that, they all wave and nod at each other. This warmth is also offered to outsiders, at least those who come to Lāna'i with the right attitude. In our previous meetings with Hui Mālama Pono O Lāna'i, we have been welcomed as family by Jackie Woolsey, Sol Kaopuiki, Carol Ah Toong, and the other volunteers who have made it their lifelong unpaid business to take care of Lāna'i's botanical heritage.

The Hui's attitude is typical. Stop by the Lion's Club eye clinic, the Senior Citizens' 'ukulele performance, or the Little League baseball game, and you will probably be welcomed and fed. Visit the Blue Ginger Cafe, the laundromat, the Pine Isle Market, or the Dis N' Dat Shop and someone will inevitably strike up a conversation with you. And talk to people long enough, and they will also tell you about the past.

Settled by Polynesians in the 1400s, Lāna'i was a true pawn and doormat in the more sweeping interisland wars that raged across the Hawaiian chain. Legends tell of battles, banishments, and rivalries and of an ancient priest who kept a perpetual bonfire burning to safeguard the island's fertility. In 1778, though, just a few months before the arrival of Captain James Cook, an army led by Kamehameha slaughtered most of the population and burned much of Lāna'i to the ground.

It is plantation history, however, that links people together today. At the turn of the last century, the Lāna'i Ranch Company consolidated its land holdings and invested in sugar and cattle. Neither succeeded to any great extent, but pineapple did. Through the efforts of James Dole and his successors Lānaʻi eventually became the world's largest pineapple plantation.

Today, even though the pineapple fields are gone, Lānaʻi is one of the last places in Hawaiʻi where those plantation traditions still weave into everyday mannerisms. As they did seventy years ago, people celebrate each others' holidays. They go to the Hongwanji Church's sushi sale, the annual open house at the hospital, the Rizal Day celebration, and the Filipino Lantern parade. Everyone eats everyone else's food. And most everyone goes to bed early and rises at the crack of dawn.

Most of all, everyone minds everyone else's business. Each day, people stop by the post office or "Old Man's Park" in the middle of Lānaʻi City to talk about fishing, hunting, and the comings and goings of other Lānaʻians. If it's Thursday, people will inevitably wander down to Kāmalapau Harbor to watch the barge come in. And as a matter of course, everyone automatically watches over everyone else's children. If a kid wises off, he or she can count on two good scoldings, one from the neighbors and then again at home.

On Lānaʻi, civic life runs almost exclusively on volunteer energy. There are no professional city managers and no complaint departments. Groups like Hui Mālama Pono O Lānaʻi form up to do what needs to be done, whether it be repainting the hospital, cleaning culverts, or organizing adult education classes. Personal responsibility, mutual support, and little acts of "aloha" are a continuous way of life.

This is not to say that things on Lānaʻi are perfect. As in any other small town, there are feuds and grudges and fierce political debates. There are people who hate the two new world-class, five-star hotels that have been built at Kōʻele and Mānele Bay and others who love them. There are newcomers who fit right in and old-timers who never did. Nonetheless, Lāna'i is a real community. People mingle, interact, and have a detailed mental map of who belongs and who doesn't.

We drive through Lāna'i City and see people working in their front-yard gardens. We pass two little boys playing inside a doghouse (while the dog anxiously looks on). We drive through the town center and slide by the community college, the police station, the jail (a converted meat locker), and some newly built senior homes painted in pastels. Then, seven and one-half minutes after entering Lāna'i City, we are out the other end of it on one of Lāna'i's many dirt roads.

Three or four miles across a rutted road and close to the top of the island's western plateau, we come to the grove of trees we have come here to see: Kānepu'u Reserve. Held in trust by The Nature Conservancy, this tiny, fenced sanctuary represents most of the last remaining 2 percent of a type of forest that once covered the dry lowland slopes of Maui, Lāna'i, and Moloka'i. The fact that it is here at all is the legacy of a New Zealander named George C. Munro, who came to the island in 1911 to manage the Lāna'i Ranch Company's operations.

Munro was one of a kind, a tough and skillful cattleman, an avid ornithologist, and a dedicated conservationist who loved the "Back of Beyond." Even as he set out to make the ranch profitable, he studied every facet of Lāna'i's natural history. He discovered new species, checked the erosion that had carried off much of the island's topsoil, and halted the indiscriminate proliferation of feral animals.

Today, Munro's efforts are remembered by the birds that are named after him, by a road and ridge trail that bear his name, and by an important historical manuscript called *The Story of Lāna'i*. The reserve at Kānepu'u and the work that Jackie, Sol, Carol, and others are doing is also part of his legacy.

Stripped to its essence, Kānepuʻu is a small, windblown island of *lama* (native ebony) and *olopua* (native olive) sheltered by a large fence that keeps the deer out. In turn, the *lama* and *olopua* provide cover for forty-five other native plants. Each month, members of the Hui, along with Brian and others from The Nature Conservancy, spend time tending this living link to Lānaʻi's past. The area surrounding Kānepuʻu is severely eroded and full of weeds.

We walk through the grove and Brian shows us some of its treasures. A rare sandalwood. The Hawaiian tree gardenia. A vine named *Bonamia menziesii*. As in Munro's time, we do what we can in the time that we have. We check the fence for holes, water a few plants, pull some weeds, set some rattraps, pick up discarded soda cans, and then start back to Lānaʻi City.

On the way back and on the outskirts of Lānaʻi City, Brian slows down. In front of us two drivers going in opposite directions have stopped and are blocking the way. Leaning on sun-darkened arms, the two men, both wearing baseball caps, have turned off their engines and are smoking cigars and having a long chat. One of them smiles and waves at us. Brian kills the engine. A car backs up behind us. Then another car stacks up in the opposite lane. Nobody on Lānaʻi has ever heard of road rage. Nobody gets edgy. Nobody honks.

Back in Lānaʻi City, we meet with members of the Hui and then visit friends. After an early dinner, we head to the airport and board the plane with several hunters. One of them is carrying a set of antlers. Another has a cooler full of venison.

We settle into the DASH-8 as the sun is starting to set. Then, when we are aloft, the steward comes down the aisle wishing everyone a good evening and passes out small plastic cups of pineapple-orange punch.

Habits of the Heart

aisy Cachero grew up in a dusty little plantation
town called Kamakani on the west side of Kaua'i.
Her grandparents came to Hawai'i from the province
of Ilocos Norte in the Philippines to work on the sugar plantations. Like others who came before them from China and
Japan, the Cacheros thought that they would eventually return
to their birthplace. Instead, they stayed. Today, the Islands are
unquestionably and indisputably their home.

Kem Lowry, my golfing mentor and husband of sushi mentor Junko Lowry, is a professor of urban and regional planning
at the University of Hawai'i. A quiet, thoughtful man, he grew
up in Valley Falls, Kansas. After a three-year stint in the Peace
Corps in Malaysia, he moved to Hawai'i to do his graduate stud-
ies. He too thought he would leave Hawai'i after he earned his
Ph.D., but he, Junko, and their son Cameron wouldn't think
of living anyplace else.

Hi'ilei Silva is a volunteer teacher at the Honowai Elementary School in Waipahu. "Eur-Asian" is too limited a word to
describe Hi'ilei. She is Hawaiian, Chinese, English, Tahitian,

Spanish, Filipina, and Chicasaw Indian. Hiʻilei's family tree has multiple branches, but one part of her ancestry tracks back to those first seafarers who found Hawaiʻi fifteen centuries ago under the star called Arcturus.

Daisy, Kem, and Hiʻilei are all residents of the 50th State. All three of them have deep roots in the community. They love Hawaiʻi, partake of its rich civic life, cherish its breathtaking environment, and thrive on the gentle multiculturalism that permeates everyone's daily habits. For all intents and purposes, we should consider Daisy, Kem, and Hiʻilei "local."

Or should we?

In a place where everyone originally came from somewhere else, the word "local" carries curious and sometimes controversial meanings. Many people use the term to describe someone who is from the Islands and went to a local high school. Others argue that only *kanaka maoli* can be considered local because they were the first people to come here. And still others say it is all about the little customs and conventions of daily life on a mid-Pacific island.

From time to time when I'm in a philosophical mood I ponder these different points of view. Being local, after all, is all about belonging. At some fundamental level, it is linked to who we are, where we think of as "home," and how we view our circumstances in life. To some people, "place" is inextricably a part of personality. To others, it is simply a piece of the passing panorama, the spot they happen to be walking on at the moment.

One person who has studied this matter for several years is my friend Chris Leong. Chris is a 46-year-old Chinese psychologist who grew up in the Islands and did his Ph.D. work in this area. He read everything he could on the subject, conducted surveys, organized focus groups, and then performed in-depth interviews with island residents. The results of all his mulling are lodged in a dissertation called "You Local or What? An Exploration of Identity in Hawai'i."

Chris sees several patterns. The first and most prevalent is the "born and raised in Hawai'i" idea that equates "local" to how long a person has been here. A second concept is grounded in culture and ethnicity. This definition usually refers to people whose ancestries trace back to Polynesia or Asia. The third concept, he observes, has to do with language and lifestyle. "People are identified as local if they speak pidgin, dress casually, and demonstrate an understanding of Hawai'i's different cultures."

Over the years Chris and I have maintained a vigorous running conversation on this topic, most often sitting on my back deck on Sunday afternoons nursing a couple of beers. Chris is an engaging man, considerate to talk to, and the very first to admit that the "who is local" question is a tricky bit of business. And he also acknowledges that Hawai'i has its own code of everyday definitions, many of which come straight from the kitchen.

Telltale signs are relishing things like adobo, chicken *heka,* and tripe stew. Other observable evidence includes measuring the water for rice with the knuckle of an index finger and cracking a raw egg over it when it emerges fresh and hot from the rice cooker. Local people also keep a serious army of condiments handy to go with these meals: soy sauce, rock salt, kimchi, chili pepper water, pickled onions, sliced turnips, vinegar, and several varieties of fish flakes that mainland people equate with the fish and turtle food you buy at pet stores.

Foot behavior offers another set of indicators. People from Hawai'i always take their shoes off when they enter a house and they will nearly always drive barefoot, even if they happen to be on the mainland. You will also notice that local people often wear two different slippers and have slipper tans in the form of an upside-down "v" on the top of their feet. But the true test comes when a rubber thong breaks. Local people know 101 ways to fix them, fifty using tape, fifty with glue, and one using a pair of chopsticks.

Being local is revealed in other ways. Daisy Cachero says that when people from Hawai'i travel to and from other islands, they always bring back a specialty from each place. It might be black bean pastries from Maui, Portuguese sweet bread from O'ahu, dried fish from Hilo, or guava cookies from Kaua'i. All of this interisland purchasing and hauling has a secondary motive. Local people never, ever go to anyone else's house without bringing *omiyage,* a small gift that signifies friendship and respect.

Kem Lowry discerns some other traits that have to do with unique and everyday knowledge. He thinks local people have their own built-in clocks, calendars, and maps. They always know exactly which market sells the best poi on what days and which days Char Hung Sut (one of Hawai'i's premier *manapua* shops) is closed. They call surf spots by their colloquial names ("Pounders," "Sandy's," "Walls") and they have no idea about true distances and directions. Things are either "near" or "far," *"mauka"* or *"makai."*

With humor and gentleness, Chris sees most of these little clues as quirky and valid but indicative of something deeper. One of his core findings is that anyone can become "local" if he or she has the right outlook on life. "There are people who recently moved to the Islands and quickly acquire a local status," he insists. "There are others who were born and raised in Hawai'i who never will." The difference, he is convinced, is personal attitude.

Hi'ilei Silva couldn't agree more. She passionately believes that the true essence of being local is doing everything with aloha. She works hard to impart this when she teaches hula and Hawaiian culture to the elementary students at Honowai

School. "Aloha isn't just a phrase we use to say hello and goodbye. It's an expression of great caring. It is the way we convey deep respect and love for each other and for our island home."

There is one other notion of localness that bears mention here. Call it the "Local-Is-As-Local-Does" theory in commemoration of several recent and memorable caucuses with Chris on the back deck. The premise is deceptively simple.

"Local" isn't a set of immutable traits or characteristics. Nor does it have anything to do with the place you happened to be born or intend to die. Instead of being a "thing" that resides inside people like a ligament or a pancreas, it is a small and perishable magic that unfolds in everyday settings and ordinary ways. Local, it turns out, is neither noun nor adjective. It is a verb.

The best way to comprehend this is to watch people from Hawai'i as they congregate on weekends. The place you choose to do this might be a neighborhood slow-pitch baseball game in the Kaimukīneighborhood or over in the 'Aiea community as a gaggle of volunteers with hammers and saws rebuild a termite-eaten bus shelter. It might be a sun-drenched canoe race at Hanalei or a rodeo in the cool up-country town of Makawao. It could be at the farmer's market in downtown Hilo where buyers and sellers negotiate over fresh produce or it might be at the Diamond Head Arts Festival where people will stand around for hours discussing the merits of *raku* pots and handwoven hats.

But mainly, you want to go to the parks. There, you will scan the grassy strands above the shoreline and see local families knotted together in little groups. In some cases, you will see that these seemingly separate groups are threaded together as if they were part of a giant flower lei. You will, of course, see many different kinds of local folks enjoying the afternoon and, if you look carefully, you will probably see my people also.

Most of these are my in-laws, the Watanabe clan. Presided over by Grandpa Tetsui and Grandma Alice, who are in their 80s, it includes my wife, Carolyn, her four brothers and sisters, a huge assortment of husbands, wives, kids, and grandkids, and at least a half dozen friends and visitors who have been incorporated into the tribe for what may turn out to be a few hours or a few years or forever.

Look closer, and you soon notice that several people at the Watanabe gathering are Caucasians like me. So too are Tom, Julie, and Carol. You will also see Okinawans like KC's wife, Gail, her brother Dale, and their mom, Aunty Ruth. Later, you will meet Carolyn's cousin Ted, who is married to Connie, a Filipina, and you will look at our kids, some of whom are "hapa-haole" Asians with blond hair, and others of whom have faces that could be Tibetan, American Indian, or Tiger Woods.

During the course of a long afternoon, there will be some swimming, newspaper and spy novel reading, and Scrabble playing. Long snoozes on tatami mats are inescapable. Babies will be passed around and gossip will be exchanged. Projects will be discussed, parties will be planned, and opinions about little local scandals will be savored. At various times (and sometimes continuously), great piles of home-cooked food will be devoured. In addition to a lot of talking, people are gobbling down barbecued beef sticks, baked tofu, pickled cucumber and cabbage, five-bean salad, fresh sashimi dipped in wasabi, miso pork, cake-fried noodles, smoked fish, *kālua* pig, Korean-style shortribs, sushi, sweet potatoes, bananas and papayas, guava jam meringue squares, and mango nut cake. There will also be a few beers in the cooler.

All of this eating, lounging around, and palavering is called "talking story," which is not, strictly speaking, about talking or about stories. It is an alchemy peculiar to Hawai'i, a special way in which the bonds of family, friends, and community are maintained and perpetually renewed. Everyone eventually comes to the conversation. Everyone brings something special. Everyone participates. It all blends together.

The same thing will be happening a few picnic tables away where the Lowrys, the Cacheros, the Leongs, and the Silvas may be gathering with their people. The key is relishing small and simple things, moving at a slightly slower pace than the rest of humanity, and exercising continuous reciprocity. On islands, people share with each other tangibly because they are tied to each other by a small common ground and a large, circular horizon that makes such bonds inescapable.

In Hawai'i, these habits of the heart seem casual, but they aren't. They are easygoing only because they are practiced regularly. It is our way of doing things, something those who stay for awhile come to understand and love. When they do, they too become part of the oxtail soup that blends us together while retaining those special little flavors that make each of us different.

A Guide to Some Hawaiian Words and Place Names in *Oxtail Soup*

'a'ā. A rough and jagged form of lava.

'a'ali'i. Several species of native hardwoods, both shrubs and trees.

'Āina Haina. A neighborhood in East Honolulu.

Alaka'i. A swamp and trail near Waimea on the island of Kaua'i.

'apapane. A crimson-colored member of the Hawaiian honeycreeper family.

Duke Kahanamoku Beach. The beach in front of the Hilton Hawaiian Village Hotel in Waikīkī.

'Ewa. A plantation town and district near Pearl Harbor.

Hakalau. A wildlife refuge on the slope of Mauna Kea.

hala. The pandanus or screw pine, native across South Asia and the Pacific.

Halapē. Name of a trail and cove in the Ka'ū Desert region of Hawai'i Volcanoes National Park.

Hanalei. A land section, village, and river on Kaua'i.

Hanaʻula. A 4,616-foot peak in the West Maui mountains.

haole. White person, American, Englishman, Caucasian. Sometimes used derogatorily.

hāpuʻu. An endemic tree fern common in many of Hawaiʻi's forests.

Hilina Pali. A cliff overlooking the desert section of Hawaiʻi Volcanoes National Park.

Hōkūleʻa. The star Arcturus and the name of an open-ocean Polynesian sailing canoe.

ʻilima. A shrub bearing delicate flowers prized by lei makers.

Kahuku. A town and land division on the northernmost point of Oʻahu.

Kaluakauka. A memorial near the spot where David Douglas died.

Kāmalapau Harbor. The main shipping port on the island of Lānaʻi.

Kamehameha. The name of a succession of Hawaiian kings.

Kānepuʻu. A small nature preserve on the island of Lānaʻi.

Kapua. An ancient land area in Waikīkī, now filled and part of Kapiʻolani Park.

Kealakomo. A land division and ancient village in the Puna District on the island of Hawaiʻi.

kiawe. The algaroba tree, a legume from Peru.

Kīlauea. An active volcano on the island of Hawaiʻi.

Kilohana. Name of a land division and a gulch and peak on Kauaʻi.

koa. A native tree, prized by woodworkers.

Kōkeʻe. A state park on Kauaʻi.

Kokokahi. Name of a neighborhood, lit. "one blood."

Koʻolau Mountains. A mountain range on Oʻahu.

Kua Pāpā Loʻi O Kānewai. An area of taro patches in Mānoa Valley.

kukui. The candlenut tree.

Kuluʻī. A street in ʻĀina Haina named for certain small trees and shrubs.

Laupāhoehoe. A land area and small town on the island of Hawaiʻi.

lei. Flowers strung in a circle and presented to friends and guests.

lilikoʻi. Purple water lemon or granadilla.

luakini. A temple where chiefs prayed and human sacrifices were offered.

Māʻalaea. A harbor on Maui.

maile. A fragrant native twining shrub found in the forest and used by lei makers.

Mānoa. A valley in Honolulu.

Mauna Kea. Highest mountain (nearly 14,000 feet) in Hawaiʻi.

Mōhihi. An area near Waimea Canyon on Kauaʻi.

mokihana. A native citrus tree found only on Kauaʻi with anise-scented fruits.

Nāpuʻuonāʻelemākule. Coastal hills in the volcanoes region of the island of Hawaiʻi, lit. "The Hills of the Old Men."

ʻōhiʻa. Name of several kinds of trees found in Hawaiʻi's forests.

ʻōkolehao. A homemade liquor distilled from the root of the ti plant.

Onekahakaha. A beach and beach park near Hilo.

pāhoehoe. A smooth billowy and ropy flow of lava.

pīkake. Arabian jasmine, introduced from India.

pili. A native grass used for thatching houses.

Poʻipū. A land division and beach on Kauaʻi.

Ponahawai. Name of a street in Hilo, lit. "water circle."

pūkiawe. A native shrub, common in the volcano region on Hawaiʻi.

Puna. A district and land section on the island of Hawaiʻi.

Pūpūkea. A beach area on the North Shore of Oʻahu.

Puʻukapukapu. A mountain in the Kaʻū Desert region of Hawaiʻi Volcanoes National Park.

Puʻu Kukui. West Maui's highest spot.

Puʻu o ʻUmi. A hill on Maui and a forest reserve on Hawaiʻi.

San Souci. A beach between Diamond Head and Waikīkī.

Ukumehame Valley. A steep, seldom-visited valley on Maui.

ʻulu maika. Stones used in a game similar to bowling.

Violet Lake. A small lake in the West Maui mountains.

Waiʻaleʻale. Highest peak on Kauaʻi.

Wailoa River. A land section and river in Hilo on the island of Hawaiʻi.

Waimea. Name of a canyon and town on Kauaʻi.

Wainiha. A land section, village, and river on Kauaʻi.

About the Author

Peter S. Adler lives and works in Honolulu. He is married to Carolyn Watanabe, has three daughters, and is a partner in The Accord Group, LLC, an international consulting firm specializing in planning, facilitation, and conflict resolution. He is the author of *Beyond Paradise* (Ox Bow Press, 1993) and was a contributing editor for *ISLANDS* Magazine from 1996 to 1999.